HENRY J. KAUFFMAN

# Early American Ironware

## Cast and Wrought

WEATHERVANE BOOKS NEW YORK

# Contents

# Illustrations

9

# Acknowledgments

IT IS INTERESTING TO NOTE THAT the last act of an author in writing a manuscript, the listing of the names of persons and organizations who have contributed to his project, should be placed at the beginning of the book. The incongruity of the procedure probably arises from the fact that in this way the author wishes to acknowledge his debts, and he thinks this can best be done by placing the names of the contributors where they are most likely to be seen and read. Such compensation is surely inadequate for their unselfish help, but until a better plan of recognition is devised, I will continue the practice.

A survey the size of this one could not be made by one person. The individuals and organizations which I list below have shared significantly in its preparation, however, the author is completely responsible for any inaccuracies or omissions. I would like to record my grateful thanks to the following individuals and organizations.

Miss Dorothy C. Barck
Mr. John T. Butler
Mr. John DuMont
Mr. Samuel E. Dyke
Mr. John J. Evans
Mr. Frank Ewing
Dr. Kathryn Fennely
Dr. Reginald French
Mrs. H. C. Fredrick, Jr.
Mr. Francis C. Haber
Mr. Charles Hanson

Mr. Luther Heisey
Mr. Frank Horton
Mr. Charles Hummel
Mr. Joe Kindig, Jr.
Mr. Ernest Ludhe
Mrs. Frank Mish, Jr.
Mr. Harold Peterson
Mrs. Josephine Pierce
Mr. Frank Spinney
Mr. Donald Streeter
Mr. M. W. Thomas

Mr. Samuel Wilson, Jr.

American Antiquarian Society
American Iron and Steel Institute
Buffalo Historical Society
Colonial Williamsburg
Essex Institute
Franklin Institute
The Historical Society of Pennsylvania
The Historical Society of York County
Hopewell Village

The Lancaster County Historical Society
The Maryland Historical Society
The Massachusetts Historical Society
The Metropolitan Museum
National Park Service
New Jersey State Museum
New York Historical Society
Pennsylvania Historical and Museum
   Commission
Saugus Iron Works
Sleepy Hollow Restorations

# Introduction

A PICTORIAL SURVEY OF OBJECTS made of iron in America and the trades that produced them might be logically prefaced with some historical and technical data that influenced their production. As a result, an understanding of the factors that controlled the production of iron objects might lead to a fuller appreciation of their qualities and a recognition of their importance to the economy of the society in which they were used.

It is interesting to note that on both sides of the Atlantic there was an almost simultaneous development in the facilities for producing iron and objects of iron. This situation belies the tradition that the technology of early America lagged behind that of Europe. There are a number of explanations for this unusual condition in the iron industry of the 17th and 18th centuries.

It is obvious that the invention of the blast furnace was contemporary with the discovery and the colonization of the New World. Agricola does not mention a blast furnace in his monumental book on metallurgy, *De Re Metallica,* published in 1556; yet within less than a century, two blast furnaces were built on American soil. The facts suggest that the furnace was a new invention and that enterprising Europeans had little opportunity to send plans for an obsolete model to America. It should also be pointed out that over a long span of years, technicians were sent to America who were experienced in the best procedures for refining ore. Since there was a great demand for pig iron in England, there was nothing to be gained by sending second-class men here to produce this important commodity. The production of a supply of pig iron from America fitted the contemporary English scheme of mercantilism. English merchants hoped to get iron from America from which they could fabricate objects and resell them to their colony. However, it never occurred to them that the development of the colony's rich natural resources would eventually contribute to its rebellion and freedom, to the establishment of a new nation with new ideals, a new culture, and an individuality that was unique. The artifacts and the story of their production are the subject of this survey.

17

Plate 1. *Architectural plan for the restoration of the First Iron Works at Saugus, Massachusetts. The iron master's house is located at the far left, the blast furnace left of center, and the finery-forge to the right. The largest of the three buildings in the foreground is the rolling and slitting mill. The other buildings are subsidiary to the main plant. (Courtesy of the First Iron Works Association)*

Plate 2. *Soft, surface deposit of bog iron ore being worked by pick and shovel during Colonial days. (Courtesy of the American Iron and Steel Institute)*

# CHAPTER ONE

# The Blast Furnace

SOON AFTER, A PERMANENT SETtlement was established in Virginia, an English society of merchants sponsored the building of a furnace for producing iron there. Sixty-six miles from Jamestown, at a site called Falling Creek, men toiled for several years erecting a furnace. They were plagued with troubles, principally Indian raids, so that a company of militia had to be sent to protect them while they worked. On March 22, 1622, a trial was to be made and everything was prepared to celebrate the day when the furnace would be first operated; ore and fuel were obtained, and sea shells were piled high to provide limestone for the operation. Unfortunately, at the moment the furnace was to be lighted, the Indians expressed their disapproval of the project by attacking, destroying the furnace, and killing all but three of the white people. This experience was so discouraging that twenty years passed before a similar venture was attempted, this time at Saugus, Massachusetts, and the New World began

fulfilling its promise of iron from native ores.

The project in Massachusetts owed its inception to John Winthrop, Jr., who came to Massachusetts to join his father, the colony's first governor. His scientific knowledge led him to serious investigations of the bog-ore in the region, which resulted in a trip to England, where he was successful in raising capital and organizing the "Company of Undertakers for the Iron Works in New England." In 1643, Winthrop sailed from England with his capital and equipment, but he arrived late in the fall, and the actual beginning of operations had to be delayed until a more favorable time. The company received a twenty-one year monopoly from the local court, as well as certain restrictions, exemptions from taxes, and the right to export iron after local needs were met.

In subsequent years, a fair-sized operation was developed; however, it was always dogged with troubles. In 1645, Winthrop

was replaced by Richard Leader, who had some experience and "skill in mynes and the tryall of metals." In August, 1648, Governor Winthrop wrote his son that the furnace was then producing seven tons of metal a week; and a month later, he reported that the furnace was running eight tons a week. In 1650, Leader resigned and was replaced by John Gifford, an experienced iron worker from Europe, and great expectations were held for the future. A great deal of money was spent for the accommodation of additional workmen who were brought over from Europe and certain unwarranted expenses were incurred, so that Gifford was finally thrown into jail. The employees were constantly charged with infractions such as swearing, drunkenness, adultery, and violation of the Sabbath. There was friction between the operators of the furnace and the English shareholders; but despite all their troubles, the furnace produced some iron. From 1658, when William Paine bought the controlling interest in the furnace, until 1663, more than three-hundred tons of iron were produced. In 1676, the plant became the property of Samuel Appleton; but so complete was the disrepair that two years later it was abandoned, and local residents petitioned the court to clear away the dam in the Saugus River.

For almost three hundred years this furnace and its appendages, covered with many feet of fill and debris, were forgotten. The attempted removal of the ironmaster's house sparked a new movement, and deliberate steps were taken by interested people to save the house and restore the furnace. Subsequent excavations revealed seven water wheels and a large number of artifacts, including the iron hammer of the forge. There is evidence that about 1650 the plant consisted of an ironmaster's house, a blast furnace, a forge, a slitting mill, a wharf, and a waterway. The ironmaster's house is the only original building left at the site; however, the others have been rebuilt with the architectural and technological fidelity that should be the rule in such an important project. The water runs in the spillway, and the bellows are in location to produce a blast; the forge and the slitting mill stand on their original sites, perhaps on the original foundations. This interesting reproduction of the seventeenth century is a mecca for all who are interested in seeing how iron was made at that time. The original furnace produced a large quantity of pig iron and a sizeable number of pots and kettles, but only one three-legged kettle has survived for connoisseurs to see what was made at Saugus.

There were furnaces in states adjoining Massachusetts. Connecticut's first governor, the aforementioned John Winthrop, Jr., soon turned his attention to the development of an iron industry in the state. The quantity and quality of the ore in the Salisbury region were outstanding, and over the years many furnaces were fed by it. The first furnace was built at Lime Rock and another was built at the same time at Lakeville on the shores of Lake Wononscopomus.

Two other furnaces were erected in the Salisbury region, the Chapinville being built about 1825, and the Sage Furnace at an unknown date. Others followed, such as the Scovill and Buena Vista at Caanan, both of which took their power from the Hollenback River. The industry reached its height in the early part of the nineteenth century. It is a matter of record that twenty-seven blast furnaces, as well as a number of forges and puddling furnaces, operated within thirty miles of the original Salisbury Mine.

The earliest iron works in New York

state was Ancram, having started operations in the mid 1740's with ore from the Salisbury "orehill." Its owner, Philip Livingston, had ore carted from the mine to the furnace, and in the same way the bar iron was transported to the Hudson, where it was placed on sloops and shipped to New York City. The following advertisement appeared in the *New York Weekly Journal,* April 2, 1744:

LIVINGSTON'S FORGE—To be sold by Robert Livingston Junr. A parcel of choice pig iron, at eight pound per ton. Ready money, or rum, sugar, molasses at Market Price. N.B. It's manufactured at Ancram Manner of Livingston.

The Sterling Works was also erected in the mid 1740's and was twice the size of the Ancram Works. An anchor of 1450 pounds is known to have been made there, and the following notice in the *New York Gazette* and *Weekly Mercury,* April 17, 1769, indi-

Plate 4. *Reconstruction of one of the massive water wheels at the First Iron Works at Saugus, Massachusetts. (Courtesy of the First Iron Works Association)*

Plate 5. *Stove pattern used by the Batsto Furnace (1766-1854) in Burlington County, New Jersey, on the Batsto River. The art of making iron stoves decorated with pictures and designs in very low relief was brought to the Colonies from Germany. The plates—heavy, rectangular, and about two feet square—are relics of charcoal blast furnaces, cast in open sand molds, and date to the early 18th century. (Photo by N. R. Ewan, from the New Jersey State Library Collection)*

cates that there were special facilities there for such production:

The Sterling Anchory, which burnt down May 1767, is rebuilt, and carried on by Noble and Townsend; all Gentlemen, Merchants, and others that will be kind enough to apply to William Hawkhurst, in New York, may be supplied with Anchors warranted a year, made of refined iron from Sterling pigs.

Its most dramatic production, however, was the iron for the chain that was stretched across the Hudson River at West Point in 1778 to impede the passage of British ships. The furnace was able to meet competition until about 1900, when it also fell prey to the more efficient large-scale production elsewhere.

Another New York furnace was built at Cortlandt by Peter Hansenclever, who came to America from England with large sums of money for the development of resources here. His large iron holdings included four furnaces, seven forges, and the other buildings that were typical of an eighteenth century iron plantation. He was one of the furnace owners in New Jersey, where he owned the Ringwood and Charlottenberg Works. An interesting notice about the Charlottenberg Furnace appeared in the September 17, 1772, issue of the *New York Journal* or the *General Advertiser:*

Ore carters for Charlottenberg Furnace. Notice is hereby given to those who usually cart ore from Hibernia mine to the above furnace, or others, that those who choose to commence carting on or about the 10th of October next, and who shall deliver a quantity not less than three tons a week, till it amounts to 3 tons, shall be paid as formerly, 10s. 6d. New York money per ton; and for their further encouragement, they shall have the same price in sleighing time. Those who begin carting after October 10 will receive 10s. per ton and if the quantity carted amounts to 20 tons, they shall receive 9s. per ton in sleighing time.

N.B. None except those who cart at the above rates, shall have the priviledge to sleigh at the foregoing prices; all others who only sleigh, are desired to remember that no more than 8s. per ton will be given at sleighing time. If through unavoidable misfortune, the carters shall fall short of their stipulated quantity, they may depend on all reasonable indulgence from the manager.                          ROBERT ERSKINE

Other famous New Jersey Furnaces include the Hibernia, Hanover, Vesuvius, Mt. Holly, Mt. Hope, Batsto, Monmouth, Weymouth, Bloomingdale, Aetna, Oxford, Ringwood and others.

The Principio Iron Works in Cecil County, Maryland, was operating in early 1728, and a North Carolina establishment advertised in the *New York Gazette and Weekly Mercury*, September 28, 1776. The impending war easily explains the urgency of this notice:

Any persons that are well acquainted with the method of casting cannon, mortars, shells and shot, and also common sorts of hollowware such as pots and kettles, etc. and are willing to go to North Carolina, may have extraordinary encouragement by applying to the Delegate of that state in Philadelphia. The expenses of their removal will be defrayed by that state, and it is not doubted just such persons as may undertake to go will find it very easy to procure good land for themselves and families, as there are many thousands of acres of vacant land convenient to the works.

Despite a late start in the erecting of furnaces, Pennsylvania soon established itself as a leader in the production of iron in America. Its success doubtless could be attributed to a bountiful nature which had richly supplied the state with the required materials: iron-stone, limestone, and charcoal. Colebrookdale is thought to have been the first furnace built in Pennsylvania. The Cornwall mine has been in continuous operation since its opening in 1742 and in recent times, since the depletion of rich ore beds in the Great Lakes region of the United States, new deposits have been staked out by producers where early deposits had been found in Pennsylvania. There was a quick succession of other furnaces in Pennsylvania, namely: Warwick, Reading, Keiths, Durham, David Jones, Mt. Pleasant, Elizabeth, Martic, Hopewell, Roxborough, Mary Ann, Carlisle, Codorus, Windsor, Pine Grove, and others in western Pennsylvania.

The restored iron-making operation at Saugus, Massachusetts, is the only complete

Plate 6. *Restored furnace stack at Hopewell Village, Pennsylvania. The draft for this furnace was originally supplied by bellows which were replaced by the blowing tubs, located to the right of the furnace. Blowing tubs were installed in many furnaces in the 19th century because they provided a greater and more steady supply of air to the furnace. (Kauffman photo)*

Plate 7. *Eighteenth century furnaces required large quantities of charcoal which was usually made on the furnace property from vast nearby stands of virgin timber. This was cut into short lengths and stacked in the shape of an indian tepee. After the mass of wood was covered with mud and sod, it was lit and allowed to burn slowly until the wood was changed into charcoal. The draft was controlled by the small openings at the base and the larger one at the top. (Courtesy of the First Iron Works Association)*

iron-producing facility to be seen in America, but it lacks the charm of Cornwall and the partially restored furnace plantation at Hopewell Village in Berks County, Pennsylvania. The Hopewell Furnace property is an excellent example of these large plantations, some of which included thousands of acres and numerous buildings. A statement in a local newspaper indicates that at one time,

The land connected with the furnace property was 5,163 acres, principally woodland. It was a cold blast one-stack furnace. Hematite and magnetic ores were used. Fifteen thousand cords of wood were consumed annually in creating charcoal, and 170 men and boys were employed. The dwellers in this little town were iron moulders, furnacemen, woodcutters, charcoal burners, and teamsters.

Throughout the winter months, property owners, who were not employees of the furnace owner, cut wood and made charcoal for the operation of the furnace. There were also some surface mining operations nearby and a quarry for limestone, which was equally important and essential.

The blast furnace, as it belched large volumes of smoke and fire into the sky, dominated the scene. It was built against a hill, with its usual appendages of water wheel and bellows. The stacks were built of stone and were about twenty-five feet square at the base. They tapered inward toward the top and were usually thirty to forty feet high. The inner chamber was round and reached its greatest diameter about one-third of its height from the bottom. The widest area was called the bosh. From there upward, the furnace was filled with its charge of limestone, ore, and charcoal; from the bosh downward, the furnace was slowly filled with iron and slag. The ground floor around the furnace, called a casting floor, was covered with sand and was roofed. At regular intervals, the furnace was tapped and molten metal flowed through large gutters, called sows, into smaller gutters, called pigs. Part of a poem written by George H. Boker describes the appearance of the red-hot iron on the casting floor.

THE LEGEND OF THE HOUNDS
Colebrook Furnace in Cornwall stands,
Crouched at the foot of the iron lands,
The wondrous hill of iron ore
That pours its wealth through the furnace door,
Is mixed with lime and smothered in wood,
Tortured with fire till a molten flood,
Leaps from the taps to the sow below

**EARLY AMERICAN IRONWARE ✦ 24**

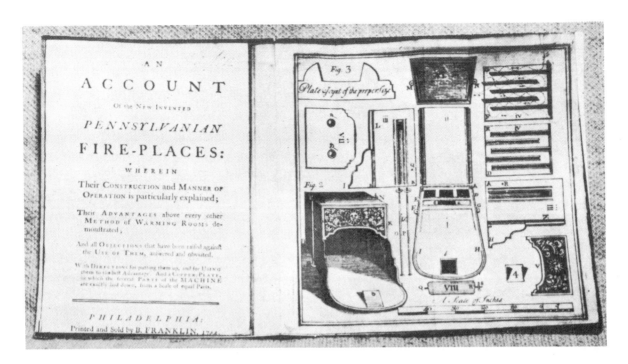

Plate 8. *Photostat of the first account of Franklin's famous fireplace. In his autobiography he noted: "In order of time, I should have mentioned before, that having, in 1742, invented an open stove for the better warming of rooms, and at the same time saving fuel, as the fresh air admitted was warmed in entering, I made a present of the model to Mr. Robert Grace, one of my early friends, who, having an iron furnace, found the casting of plates for these stoves a profitable thing, as they were growing in demand." (Courtesy Pennsylvania State Library)*

And her littered pigs that round her glow;
So that the gazer, looking down
The moulding floor from the platform's crown,
Might think, if fancy helped the spell,
He saw a grate in the roof of Hell.

At other times, or perhaps simultaneously with the casting of pigs, other objects were cast at the furnace. These include stoves, firebacks, Franklin fireplaces, cannon, cannon balls, grave markers, pipe, fences, hollow ware, and mill parts. Furnace products

Plate 9. *A cast iron five-plate jamb stove, fired from the kitchen fireplace on the other side of the wall into which it is inserted. This stove, dated 1760, was cast in Pennsylvania and bears the low-German Biblical quotation: "Las Dich Nicht Gelyssen Deines Neststen Gut," or "Thou shalt no covet thy neighbor's goods." (Courtesy of Old Salem, Inc.)*

Plate 10. *Rear view of the iron master's house at Hopewell Village, Pennsylvania. The oldest portion is to the right.*

than one time in three months. The employees occasionally attended husking parties, barn dances, or fairs, but such opportunities were limited in the remote rural areas where the furnaces were usually located. Doubtless, many workmen were tempted to run away from their life of drudgery at the furnace, and there is evidence that some of them did. The following advertisement appeared in the *Pennsylvania Gazette,* July, 1737:

### FRENCH CREEK IRON WORKS
### CHESTER COUNTY

Run away from the iron works aforesaid, a servant-man David McQuatty; by trade a Hammerer & Refiner, but has formerly followed shaloping up & down the Bay from Egg Harbor. He is a Scotchman but speaks pretty good English, middle siz'd about 28 years age of a thin visage & a little pockpetten, with a Roman nose & few spots of Gunpowder under his right eye.... Whoever secures the said servant so that the master can have him again, shall have 3 if taken up in this province, or 5 if taken up in any other province & all reasonable charges paid by
SAMUEL NUTT

The obscurity of their lives is easily evidenced by a row of unmarked head stones on the graves of workers at Martic Furnace in Lancaster County, Pennsylvania.

Plate 11. *Headstones on graves of workers at the Martic Furnace, Lancaster County, Pennsylvania. A few have initials carved on them, none have dates, and many are simply plain slabs of native stone.*

were not uniform throughout the country; for example, early New England furnaces cast firebacks and few stoves, while Pennsylvania furnaces cast many stoves but very few firebacks.

Furnaces were in blast during only part of the year: in mid-summer the heat was excessive, and in very cold weather the ice that formed on the water wheel would hamper its normal operation. It was necessary to "blow out" the furnace so that repairs could be made to the interior, which was lined with refractory stones. When the furnace was in blast, the life of the workers was one of drabness and constant labor. There was little time for relaxation; their chief diversions were gambling and drinking. It is interesting to note that an employee was to have a certain stipend for the faithful performance of his duties and a bonus of a pair of stockings if he did not get drunk more

Plate 12. *This round Stiegel stove, dated 1763, is of a very uncommon type. Stiegel also made the typical five-plate stoves at his Elizabeth Furnace at Brickerville, Pennsylvania. He later gained undying fame as a glassmaker at Manheim, Pennsylvania.*

The ironmaster lived in a large luxurious house built on the top of the hill that overlooked the furnace and all the lesser buildings. The house, in Pennsylvania, was usually built of stone, as is the one at Hopewell, and was lavishly furnished with fine furniture of the period. The ironmasters were men of great wealth and many were famous because of their participation in the political and industrial life of their day. There were frequent intermarriages in the families of these men so that the interlocking ownership of these great industries concentrated much wealth and influence in the hands of a few families. Various tales are told of their ostentatious living, such as the one about Baron Stiegel, who traveled in a costly coach with footmen and numerous horses. At the side of his coach ran a number of thoroughbred dogs; as the coach neared his residence, trumpets blared forth the news of his arrival. A spacious ballroom was located on the top floor of his mansion, where he is reputed to have entertained his community of employees at Christmas. Rich tapestries hung in his home and are now displayed at the Hershey Museum at Hershey, Pennsylvania.

Another legend tells of an ironmaster, a man of very mean disposition, given to intemperate drinking, and ruling his community with a ruthless hand. It is reported that after a very unsuccessful day in the fields with his hounds, he drove his pack up the furnace road and had workmen throw the dogs into the fiery furnace. His favorite dog cringed and quivered, but, as she licked his face, he tossed her into the flames. Residents

Plate 13. *Pair of 18th century "Hessian Soldier" andirons, probably cast in Pennsylvania or New York by German immigrants. (Courtesty of the Metropolitan Museum of Art, Gift of Mrs. Russell Sage, 1909)*

of the area contend that thereafter they could hear the barking dogs pursuing their wicked master. This incident is vividly described by George H. Boker in his poem, "The Legend of the Hounds":

A trusting, tender, loving dawn
Rose in her eyes; a low soft wail
Broke from her as the iron hand
Of the stout squire from off her stand
Swung her; and striding toward the ledge
With his pleased burden, on the edge
Of awful death—oh, foul disgrace—
She turned and licked his purple face.
Sheer out he flung her, as she fell,
Up from the palpitating hell
Came three shrill cries, and then a roll
Of thunder, Every pallid soul
Shrank from the pit; and ghastly white,
As was the snow one winter night,
The squire reeled backward. Long he gazed
From face to face; then asked, amazed,
"Was it a fancy? If you heard,
Answer was it? —that last word
Which Flora flung me?" Answer came,
as though one mouth pronounced the name,
And smote the asker as a rod:
"The word she said was—God, God, God."

In conclusion, one might point out that the blast furnaces of early America were an extremely important part of the industrial economy. The early establishment and rapid growth of the iron industry suggest that the embryo nation had a significant need for objects made of cast iron, that there was a bountiful supply of natural resources, and adequate capital to convert the resources into usable objects.

The production of iron and steel has continued from the earliest time until the present. The shape of a contemporary blast furnace closely resembles the contours of the original one at Saugus; however, the output

has been greatly increased, and the quality of the iron has been improved. These advances have made iron a comon commmodity today, so commonplace, in fact, that after a few years of use most of the objects made of iron seem to gravitate to the scrap yards.

In contrast, the objects made at the early furnaces were never in plentiful supply. It has been said that hollow ware was so scarce that a queue of buyers often stood outside a

Plate 14. *Typical cast iron grave marker in the Weymouth Burying Ground in Gloucester (now Atlantic) County, New Jersey, on the Great Egg Harbor River, cast by the Weymouth Furnace, c.1800–1862. The inscription reads: "In Memory of Rosana Ireland Babington who departed this life July 13-1825, Aged 18 months. O death it is a solemn call, A sudden judgement to us all." (Photo by N. R. Ewan, courtesy of the New Jersey State Library Collection)*

Plate 15. *Arms of England design in a fireback made of cast iron at the Oxford Furnace in 1746. The English subject indicates the strong European influence on the early products of American furnaces. (From the John M. Connor collection, courtesy of the New Jersey State Museum)*

section of furnace products is illustrated on the trade card of Joseph Webb.

BIBLIOGRAPHY

BISHOP, LEANDER J. *A History of American Manufactures from 1608 to 1860.* Philadelphia: Edward Young & Company, 1861.

BINING, ARTHUR C. *Pennsylvania Iron Manufacture in the Eighteenth Century.* Harrisburg: Pennsylvania Historical Commission, 1938.

GOTTESMAN, RITA SUSSWEIN, COMPILER. *The Arts and Crafts in New York 1726-1776.* New York: The New York Historical Society, 1938.

KEITH, HERBERT C. and HARTE, CHARLES RUFUS. *The Early Iron Industry of Connecticut.* New Haven: Mack and Noel,—

SCHUBERT, H. R. *History of the British Iron and Steel Industry from 450 B.C. to 1775 A.D.* London: Routledge and Kegan, Paul, 1957.

furnace to buy badly needed pots and pans as soon as they were produced. These objects were highly prized by the owners and were passed from one generation to another before they were discarded or "worn out."

A renewed interest in the early industrial history of America has created a great demand for the furnace products. Stoves, stove plates, and firebacks are eagerly sought by collectors and museums. A simple mortar and pestle would command high price if it could be identified as the product of a particular furnace. It is virtually impossible to distinguish between the products of the furnace and the foundry; however, some objects are inscribed with names or designs that permit positive attribution to a particular producing unit. A reasonable good cross

Plate 16. *Fireback made of cast iron at the Aetna Furnace about 1775. The attractive folk art motif indicates a departure from earlier European subjects. (Courtesy of the Metropolitan Museum of Art, Roger Fund, 1936)*

Plate 18. *The only surviving cast iron cannon of the American Revolution, displayed at the Cornwall Furnace near Lebanon, Pennsylvania. Its survival can be attributed to its imperfections for which it was rejected and never moved from the site. (Courtesy of the Republic Steel Company)*

Plate 17. *Trade card of Joseph Webb, an iron merchant in Boston, engraved by Paul Revere, which illustrates and enumerates the objects of iron he sold. (Courtesy of the American Antiquarian Society)*

Plate 19. *Page one of the English Iron Act of 1750, prohibiting the erection of additional iron-forming facilities in America or any furnace for the making of steel.*

# CHAPTER TWO

# The Forge

IT HAS BEEN SAID THAT THROUGH-out the second half of the nineteenth and the first half of the twentieth century, the industrially advanced nations of the world were living in a period dominated by products made of iron and steel. Contemporary historians frequently refer to this era as the "Age of Iron and Steel." This opinion is correct; however, the conclusion should not be drawn from it that the making of iron and steel are developments of modern technology. The largescale production of iron and steel is the result of modern technological research, but iron was made in different parts of the world as long as three-thousands years ago. The great iron pillar of Delhi is thought to have been made about 912 B.C. and the Chinese are known to have levied a tax on iron as early as 700 B.C. There is evidence from tomb excavations that the Egyptians used iron at an early date and the remains of the Graeco-Roman cities of Herculaneum and Pompeii include iron grills for windows and other interesting artifacts made of this metal.

A limited supply of iron was available to primitive man from meteors. The iron content of meteors was so high that by repeated heating and pounding, a small quantity of iron could be obtained from them. The first planned production of iron from iron ore was not by a furnace, as one would suspect, but was produced in a hole dug in the side of a hill, which was filled with alternate layers of charcoal and iron ore. A horizontal hole was dug from the bottom of the cavity to the surface of the ground through which strong winds fanned the fire to a great heat. The inconstancy of the winds caused man to invent the bellows to supply a blast and the hole (or forge, as it was sometimes called) was later lined with crude forms of masonry. This device was called a Catalan Forge because it reached a high stage of development in Catalonia, Spain. This forge method of producing iron was widely used in Europe and some forges were also built in America. Their output was limited because the fuel supply could not be replenished and the metal could not be completely melted out

Plate 20. *The Saugus Ironworks Restoration at Saugus, Massachusetts, ten miles north of Boston, is a complete and authentic replica of America's first successful iron works. At this "birthplace" of the American iron and steel industry, skilled workers three hundred hears ago produced cast and wrought iron so vitally needed in the growing country. Shown, from left to right, are the wharf and warehouse, blast furnace, forge, and rolling and slitting mill. (Courtesy American Iron and Steel Institute)*

of its matrix. There was enough heat to form a pasty mass of metal, which sank to the bottom of the forge after the fire was "burned out."

In England, this mass of metal was called a bloom and the lined hole with its bellows was called a bloomery. The blooms were small and were usually lifted out of the cavity with tongs, by hand. By repeated heating in a forge and hammering on an anvil, this impure and oddly shaped mass of metal was brought to a condition of high refinement and great strength. The heat burned the carbon out of the bloom and the hammering compacted this fibrous, stringy mass into a strong bar, called wrought iron. Wrought iron was the ideal medium for the smith to use in fabricating objects, for it was tough, malleable, ductile, and very resistant to rust. The rust resistant quality of charcoal iron is attributed to the fact that sulphur was not introduced into the iron when charcoal was used to smelt the ore. In the earliest times, blooms were hammered by hand, but later,

for this lengthy and important operation, the hammer was raised by water power.

There are records of men having found outcroppings of rich iron ore on the earth's surface in New England and Pennsylvania, and in the latter area, it is known that some bloomeries were built. There is a record in 1717 that,

This last summer one Thomas Rutter, a smith, who lives not far from Germantown, hath removed further up in the country and his own strength hath set about making iron. Such it proves to be highly set by, by all the smiths here, who say that Swede's iron doth not exceed it, and we have heard of others that are going on with the iron works. It is supposed there is stone (ore) sufficient for ages to come—and in all likelihood hemp and iron may be improved and transported home—. If not discouraged.

This statement suggests that it was expedient to build a small inexpensive bloomery to determine the extent of a deposit, or that it was financially feasible to build a small unit before an expensive furnace should be built.

The large forges associated with the

Plate 21. *Architectural drawing of the forge at Saugus, Massachusetts. Many details are hypothetical inasmuch as no American forge has survived to serve as a model for such a building. (Courtesy of the First Iron Works Association)*

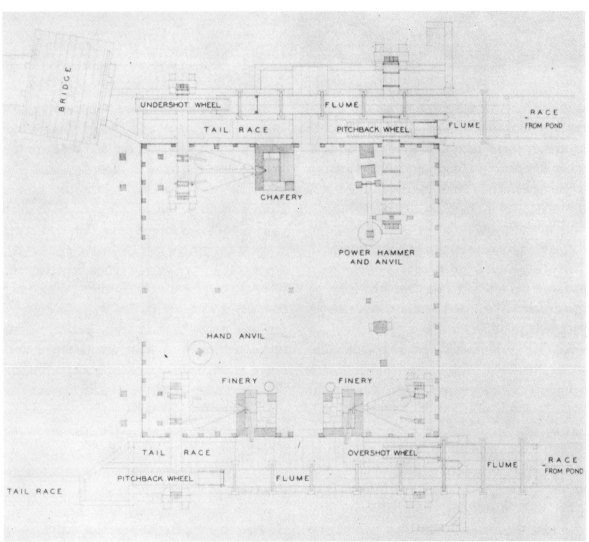

Plate 22. *Floor plan of the forge at the First Iron Works Restoration at Saugus, Massachusetts. The major equipment consists of two fineries, one chafery, and one power hammer. In this building the cast iron from the furnace was converted to wrought iron for the rolling and slitting mill. (Courtesy of the First iron Works Association)*

furnaces in America throughout the seventeenth, eighteenth and early nineteenth centuries were designed to do essentially what was done at a bloomery, but on a much larger scale. They were usually located near furnaces, for in such an arrangement the problem of moving heavy pigs of cast iron from the furnace to the forge was minimized. The great hazard inherent in the operation of forge fires dictated that the buildings be constructed of stone. The floors were earth, packed hard by much walking, and the roofs were of tile. English forges were generally about thirty feet wide and ranged in length from forty to seventy feet. The reconstructed forge building at Saugus is about thirty-five feet by forty feet.

No records dealing with the operation of forges in America have survived, but it seems safe to assume that procedures here generally followed the English pattern. The majority of English forges had two finery hearths, one chafery hearth, and one large hammer. The finery hearths were larger and deeper than the hearth of an ordinary black-smith shop and were lined with heavy plates of iron. Each finery and chafery had a water wheel which supplied the air blast for the intense heat required to melt the iron. The large hammer was also moved by power from a water wheel.

The heavy, brittle pigs of cast iron were taken from the furnace to the finery hearths, where they were slowly rolled into the fire. Here they were simultaneously melted and partially decarburized. Beads of molten iron dropped to the bottom of the hearth, where they were broken with an iron rod and raised again to the heat of the blast for further decarburizing. After the second exposure to the fire, the hot, partially softened iron was allowed to accumulate on the bottom of the hearth, where it was gathered into a ball or bloom. The bloom was again exposed to the action of the blast by raising and rotating it on an iron rod, until the operator was satisfied that most of the carbon was burned out of the iron. After the third melting, the ball was worked and kneaded until slag and other impurities no longer adhered to the

Plate 24. *Artist's sketch of the rolling mill at Saugus, Massachusetts. These small rods were probably prepared for making nails by a small-town blacksmith. (Courtesy of the First Iron Works Association)*

mass. The finer then knew that complete malleability was achieved in the bloom. The entire process of melting, refining, and balling required about an hour.

After the ball was removed from the finery with great tongs, it was beat with a sledge hammer on an iron plate to remove all the crust of charcoal and slag. It was then dragged to the great water hammer, where it was first struck lightly. Stronger blows followed until the mass was shaped into a thick square. It was then returned to the finery hearth for a final sweating out of impurities and the temperature was raised to a welding heat. When the heat was attained, the metal was taken to the water hammer, where it was forged into a bar about three feet long with knobs on each end, one larger than the other. These bars were called anconies.

The end with the small knob was then placed in the chafery fire and later forged to the same cross dimension as the middle of the bar. The bigger end required two heats to forge it until the bar was uniform from end to end.

The last operation on the forged bar was to cut off the ends, where the impurities were forced by forging from the center outward, thus making the bar as perfect as possible. In the eighteenth century, four tons of pig iron were required to produce three tons of malleable iron.

Because of the rapid cooling of a small bar of iron, the forges did not produce small bars that could be quickly and easily used by a blacksmith. This problem was solved by the invention of two devices which were often combined under one roof, a slitting and rolling mill. Some bars were reduced in size at a slitting mill by huge cutters, which acted like a giant scissors, while other bars were rolled into sheets and then cut into usable sizes. One of the special products of the slitting mill was a type of rod cut to specific dimensions for the forging of nails. All the metal was soft charcoal iron—the medium that blacksmiths used in making the various objects that museums and collectors are eagerly gathering today.

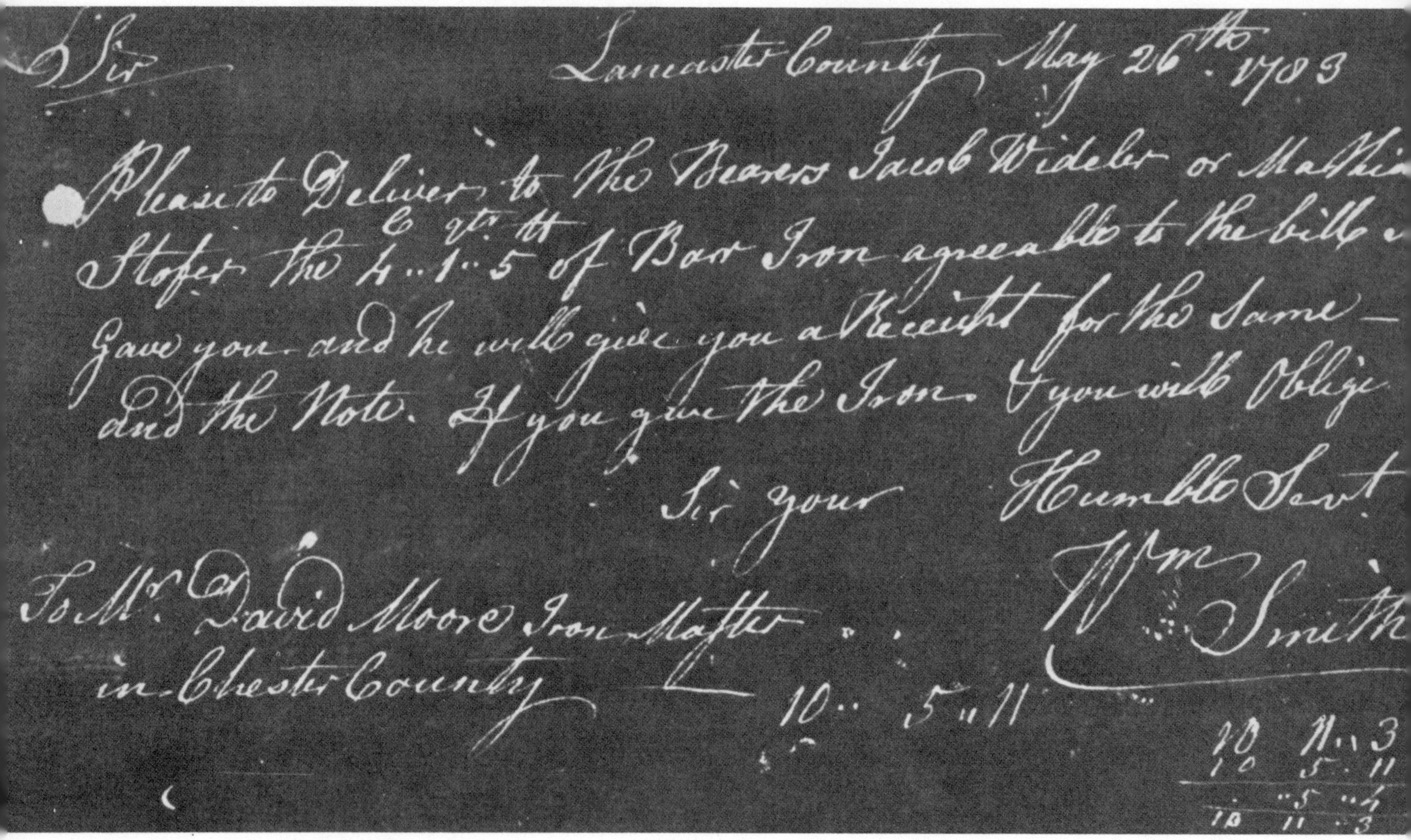

Plate 25. *Photostat of bill of sale dated May 26, 1785 for a bar of iron. Standard printed forms were not used in those days.*

BIBLIOGRAPHY

BINING, ARTHUR C. *Pennsylvania Iron Manufacture in the Eighteenth Century.* Harrisburg: The Pennsylvania Historical Commission, 1938.

SCHUBERT, H. R. *The History of British Iron and Steel Industry from 450 B.C. to 1775 A.D.* London: Routledge & Kegan Paul, 1957.

SILCOCK, ARNOLD and AYRTON, MAXWELL. *Wrought Iron and Its Decorative Use.* London & New York: Charles Scribner's Sons, 1929.

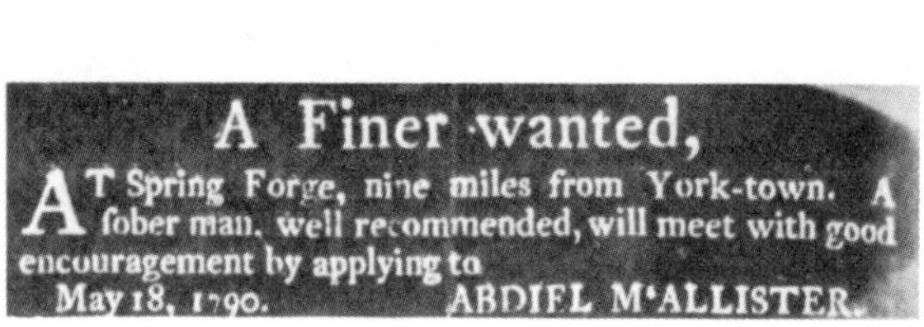

Plate 26. *Photostat of clipping from The Pennsylvania Herald and York General Advertiser, June 9, 1790.*

EARLY AMERICAN IRONWARE ✦ 36

# CHAPTER THREE

# The Iron Foundry

THE CHRONOLOGICAL HISTORY and the technological improvement of industries and trades indicate that a constant search was carried on for ways to increase the production of iron and to improve the quality of the products made of this metal. Despite significant improvements made in the operation of the blast furnace, certain inherent problems remained which were partially removed by a new device called an iron foundry.

A foundry is described in *A Dictionary of Arts, Manufactures and Mines* by Andre Ure, New York, 1856, as a place for:

the founding of metals, chiefly iron. The operations of an iron foundry consist in remelting the pig iron of the blast furnace, and giving it an endless variety of forms, by casting it in molds of different kinds, prepared in appropriate manners. Coke is the only kind of fuel employed to effect the fusion of the cast-iron.

It is not known exactly when the first foundry was operated in America, but an advertisement inserted in the *New York Daily Advertiser,* October 17, 1787, explains why foundry products were to be preferred and enumerates the objects produced at an iron foundry.

NEW YORK AIR FURNACE, Peter T. Curtenius and Co. have repaired the New York Air Furnace, and have procured the best workmen together with the necessary apparatus to carry on the Manufactory of Cast Iron in the completest and best manner. Castings made in the Air Furnace, are allowed by all who are acquainted with the nature of Founderies, to be better than that made in a Blast Furnace; because in an Air Furnace, the ware is made of the softest and best Pig Metal, and, by its being melted the second time, the scoria, or dross, is expelled and nothing but the pure metal remains. In a Blast Furnace the castings are made out of the first melting of the crude ore, and are more or less mixed with dross, which subjects the ware to be rough, spongy, and often full of cold shuts; the difference, in short, is nearly the same as there is between refined and Bloomery iron. The ware they have made is allowed, by good judges, to be as light, as smooth, and as good as any imported from Europe. This consideration alone, of the ware being as good as foreign, is a sufficient inducement for an American to give preference to the manufactures of his own country; but a more powerful argument for the purchaser to give preference is, that it can be afforded cheaper than imported ware chiefly owing to a duty of six pounds being laid on foreign castings. The ware manufactured at the Furnace, consists of the following articles, viz.

Pots and kettles of various sizes from one to fifteen gallons, tea kettles, pie pans, skillets, griddles, potash kettles and coolers, whaling kettles, boilers for tallow chandlers and sugar works, and distilleries, rollers and shears for slitting mills, chimney backs, hearth and jamb plates, cast agreeable to any pattern that may be sent; close stoves for workshops, Franklin stoves neatly decorated with carved work, Bath stoves elegantly ornamented with carvings, ships cabouses, of the new construction, with bake ovens in them, in which the same fire that roasts and boils the meat bakes the bread; mill rounds and gudgeons, saw mill cranks, calcining plates for making pearl ashes, cast iron screws for fulling and paper mills, fullers plates cast to any size that may be wanted, sash weights, forge hammers and anvils, plow plates, half hundreds, quarters, fourteen and eleven pound weights; cart, wagon, coach, phaeton, chair, and sulky boxes, etc., etc.

N.B. Persons who want any backs, or other ware cast agreeable to particular patterns, will please send their patterns and orders to the Furnace, near Mr. Atlee's Brewery or leave them at the house of Peter Curtenius No. 48, Great Dock street near the Exchange.

The construction and operation of the blast furnace and the iron foundry were in many ways similar. The foundry was essentially a smaller unit, usually located in a city, and operated on a day-to-day basis. For many years, the foundry and the furnace were highly competitive business establishments, both doing an extensive retail trade; however, the furnace finally emerged as a unit for the production of iron and the foundry became the sole producer of objects for the retail trade.

The frequent use of the word "pattern" in the advertisements of furnaces and foundries suggest that some explanation should be made concerning the use of patterns in the various metal-casting industries. The first procedure in the making of an object of cast iron was to make a pattern. They were usually made of wood, but on some occasions metal was used. They had to be perfect replicas of the object to be made and considerable skill was required of the craftsmen who made them. Pattern makers had to be well informed about procedures in foundry practice and very skilled in the working of wood. They had to have a knowledge of wood joinery and the men who carved patterns had to have skill and good taste to execute the attractive patterns used for stoves and ornamental iron work.

Some patterns were made of one piece of wood while others had to be made of a number of pieces and cleverly keyed together, so they could be removed from the sand in

Plate 27. *Cast iron tea kettle, probably 18th century, with tipping lever. By pressing down on the lever the kettle could be tipped without removing it from the fireplace. (Courtesy of the New Jersey State Library)*

**EARLY AMERICAN IRONWARE ✦ 38**

Plate 28. *Bulbous, three-legged kettles must have been a common foundry product inasmuch as they are still plentiful today. Few of them, however, are signed. This one was made by the Eagle Foundry, possibly at Lebanon, Pennsylvania. (Courtesy of Harlacker Antiques)*

which they were placed without disturbing the contour of the sand.

Much of the casting at furnaces was done on the furnace floor, which was covered with sand. Impressions of large, flat objects like stove plates could be made in the sand, into which molten metal flowed directly from the furnace. This procedure was also used at foundries to cast large objects, but the small objects were cast in sand-filled boxes, called flasks.

Flasks were rectangular boxes, without bottoms or lids, with a parting joint in the middle. The two halves had ears corresponding exactly to each other. On the one half, studs were mounted on the ears; and on the ears of the other half, holes were bored, into which the studs fitted perfectly. After sand was rammed around the pattern, the flask was parted in the middle and the pattern removed. Channels, called sprues and gates, were cut in the sand to the pattern cavity and

the flask was reassembled. The studs and holes in the ears of the two halves permitted perfect realignment when the flask parts were reassembled. Molten metal was poured from a hand ladle into the channels until the pattern cavity was filled. After the metal solidified, the castings were removed from the sand, the surfaces polished, and irregularities removed from the edges.

It was pointed out in the Curtenius advertisement that foundries produced a variety of objects ranging from pots and pans to stoves and mill parts. A building made of cast iron was erected in New York City in 1845, but it was considered a novelty and years passed before another one was built there. The discovery of gold in California created a demand for buildings which could be erected quickly. Within a short time,

Plate 29. *Cast iron tea kettle by Savery & Co. Philadelphia. This 19th century style differs from that of the 18th. (Courtesy of the Shelburne Village)*

By the middle of the nineteenth century, the great era of ornamental cast iron was flourishing in America. Robert Wood & Co. of Philadelphia became famous at this time for their products of cast iron, which they shipped to many parts of the nation. Much of their output was sold and shipped to the South, and an advertisement in the *Perry Freeman,* December 6, 1855, indicates that they were also selling some of their products in the small town of Bloomfield, Pennsylvania.

buildings of cast iron were shipped from New York City around the Horn to California. Similar buildings were shipped from England to California, but the demand for American products was greater because they could be erected in a day, whereas a month was required to erect the English products. It is evident that at this early date, America was establishing a reputation for speed that has never been relinquished.

## WOOD'S ORNAMENTAL IRON WORKS

Ridge Avenue, Philadelphia.—The attention of the public is invited to the extensive manufactory and ware-room of the subscriber who is prepared to furnish, at the shortest notice, Iron Railing, of every description for Cemeteries, Public and Private Buildings, also Verandahs, Fountains, Settees, Chairs, Lions, Dogs, etc. and other Ornamental Iron Work of a decorative character, all of which is executed with the express view of pleasing the taste, while they combine all the requisites of beauty and substantial construction.

Purchasers may rely on having all articles carefully boxed and shipped to their destination.

A book of designs will be sent to those who wish to make a selection.

ROBERT WOOD

In the same year of the Wood advertisement in the *Perry Freeman,* a local foundry was advertising objects which were obviously geared to the needs of a small agricultural community. The advertisement of the Bloomfield Foundry in Bloomfield, Pennsylvania, appeared in the *Perry Freeman* on February 15, 1855.

## BLOOMFIELD FOUNDRY

The subscriber is prepared to furnish all kinds of articles in his line of business on the shortest notice, at his Iron Foundry at the South end of Carlisle St. in Bloomfield, Perry County, Pennsylvania.

Splendid Air-Tight Parlor Stoves, Nine Plate Stoves of various patterns; and cook stoves—all of the most approved styles and patterns, are now on hand and will be kept for ready sale.

Ploughs of the most approved patterns, and Submerged Reaction water wheels of different sizes, for sale on reasonable terms.

Plate 33. *Day bed made mostly of cast iron. Although the symmetry of the end boards is not very attractive, the skirts at the front and rear, which incorporate designs of earlier wrought iron work, are very pleasing. (Courtesy of Sleepy Hollow Restorations)*

Plate 34. *Some foundries had specialties such as bells, which were used on churches, school houses, and farm buildings. (Courtesy Old Sturbridge Village)*

Plate 35. *Bells on churches were used to call people to services and to toll for deceased members of the congregation. On farm houses they were called dinner bells, being used to summon field hands to the house for their noonday meal. (Courtesy Old Sturbridge Village)*

Plate 36. *Door knocker, c.1820, of cast iron using the eagle motif that was very popular for such articles during the early days of the Republic. (Courtesy of the Metropolitan Museum of Art, Rogers Fund)*

Plate 37. *Bird houses and rustic goods made of cast iron in Baltimore. The prices (in pencil) could not have been regarded as modest at the time of the Civil War.*

Plate 38. *Cast iron parlor stove made by I. C. Potts, Albany, New York, featuring rococo revival detail of urns set in Romanesque arches. The urn on top is detachable. (Courtesy of Sleepy Hollow Restorations)*

Plate 39. *Cast iron stove with stylized floral detail, c.1850, made by E. N. Pratt and Company, Albany, New York. (Courtesy of Sleepy Hollow Restorations)*

Plate 40. *"Cook's Favorite" kitchen stove, made by Cyrus Lamborn, Chester County, Pennsylvania. It's cooking and heating facilities were versatile. There are three round openings with lids on the low fire box and two on the oven, above and behind the fire box. The oven also has two doors that are removable, making it possible to use it as a heating device for the kitchen. (Courtesy Old Salem, Inc.)*

Hollow-ware of all kinds and Mill and Machinery Gearing will be made to order with dispatch.

He has on hand every size and kind of Sled and Sleigh Soles, Wagon boxes, Kettles, Iron Washrubbers, and so forth together with many other articles in his line of business.

JAMES W. POWERS

Another famous company, known as Hayward Bartlett & Co. was located in Baltimore and, when a visitor viewed its architectural department in 1857, he reported they were making general iron work, railings, and verandahs. He also saw the iron framework for the iron roof of the Norfolk Custom House, as well as a similar one for Alexandria, each costing from $40,000 to $60,000. The same company made vacuum pans of cast iron, twenty-one feet in diameter, for evaporating salt brine. They also supplied the iron for the celebrated iron building of Harper Brothers, famous publishers in New York City.

Plates 41 and 42. *Bridge of cast iron near Ephrata, Pennsylvania, made by the Continental Bridge Company in Philadelphia and patented in 1869. Bridges were one of the various products made of cast iron in the 19th century. (Kauffman photos)*

Plate 43. *A completely naturalistic fence of cast iron in Mt. Joy, Pennsylvania. The maker's name is part of the central design in the gate. (Kauffman photo)*

Plate 44. *Cellar window grill of cast iron, Lancaster, Pennsylvania. Most cities had their own unique patterns not found elsewhere. Large cities such as Philadelphia had a number of such unique patterns. (Kauffman photo)*

chapter on "Architectural Iron Work" in *The Great Industries of the United States* published by J. Brainard, New York, 1874. Their products included:

a house, all complete, with walls, floors, doors, windows, roof, verandas, balconies, cornices, and external ornamentation of all kinds, vaults and vault lights, ventilators, fences and grates, ornamental houses, summer houses, vases, statuary, and garden sets, chairs or settees, gas and water fixtures, heating apparatus, and either kitchen ranges or cooking stoves, as required, parlor stoves or grates of any kind, ornamental brackets for shelving, hitching posts, stable fixtures, such as mangers, racks, partitions, etc., drain pipe, iron pavements, bath tubs, plumber's castings, and pipe of all kinds which go with stoves. Bedstands

In 1866, the firm name of Bartlett, Hayward & Company was changed to Bartlett, Robbins & Company. In 1868, the company was regarded as one of the most extensive manufacturers of architectural iron in the country. In 1874, their foundry shops covered three squares in Baltimore, and their size and prestige were constantly growing. Theirs was the sole firm described in the

Plate 45. *Wall bracket of cast iron, c.1850, with formalized floral detail, brightly painted in red, blue, and green. (Courtesy Sleepy Hollow Restorations)* Plate 46. *Andirons resembling cathedral spires, by Savery & Co., Philadelphia, Pennsylvania, well suited to the architectural styles of the mid-19th century. (Courtesy of The Henry Ford Museum, Dearborn, Michigan)* Plate 47. *So-called "Jenny Lind" type cast iron looking glass frame in the rococo revival style, c.1850. It was painted red, green, blue, white, and pink. (Courtesy Sleepy Hollow Restorations)*

of cast or wrought iron, or both, can also be furnished. In fact in cases of strict necessity, the firm Bartlett, Robbins & Co. could turn out a dwelling which, with the addition of the necessary textile fabrics, would be surprisingly near to complete readiness for its inmates.

It is obvious that cast iron was an important commodity in industry, in architecture, and in home furnishings in the 1860's and 70's. Its extensive use at that time is evidence that the Industrial Revolution was reaching

Plate 48. *Downspout of cast iron in the shape of a dolphin's head, found in Lancaster, Pennsylvania. (Kauffman photo)*

Plate 49. *Horsehead hitching post of the 19th century. Most foundries made these for their "city clientele." (Kauffman photo)*

Plate 50. *Few houses in the North had cast iron append-ages as extensive as this one in Lancaster, Pennsylvania. Even its door knocker and knob are of cast iron. (Kauffman photo)*

Plate 51. *A modest example of New Orleans porch ironware at the Gilmore-Ewin house, 2520 Prytania Street, New Orleans, Louisiana, built in 1853 by the architect-builder, Isaac Thayer. (Courtesy Samuel Wilson, Jr.)*

a level comparable to "high gear;" but like many other similar fashions, cast iron slowly went into decline and was replaced by mate-rials better suited to machine production.

One use for which cast iron never seems to have lost its prestige is for balconies, verandahs, or galleries, as they are called in

Plate 52. *Cast iron elements were sometimes combined in the mid-19th century Greek Revival style with wooden elements such as the pillars shown here. (Kauffman photo)*

Plate 53. *Unique trivet using Pennsylvania folk art motifs, signed on the bottom "W. B. Rimby, Baltimore, 1841." (Courtesy Osburn Collection)*

Charleston, South Carolina; but the medium certainly reached the zenith of its use in New Orleans. The Greek orders were used for columns at doorways and proportions and details are generally correct. The cast iron work in balusters, porch supports, and cornices exists in a variety of forms and details. It is an instance where decor and function are intimately interlaced and its survival and attractiveness today attest to the wisdom of its use.

The Pontalba buildings on Jackson Square were the first structures designed with cast iron galleries. The patterns for the Almonaster Pontalba Monogram were carved by a local sculptor named W. A. Talen from sketches by Madame Pontalba. The castings were made in New York City. Other castings in the city were made in the Philadelphia

New Orleans. These architectural appendages were widely used in the southern portion of the United States and many have survived as integral parts of the Greek Revival houses on which they were installed.

Architectural cast iron parts are found in many homes in the cities of Marietta, Ohio; Winston Salem, North Carolina; and

Plate 54. *Cast iron, size three mortar and pestle signed on the bottom, "Savery & Co. No. 3." The size is also indicated by the three knotches on the pestle. Many households used a mortar and pestle in the 19th century to grind spices and herbs for seasoning. The Savery foundry in Philadelphia made many household utensils of cast iron. (Kauffman Collection)*

**EARLY AMERICAN IRONWARE ✦ 48**

Plate 55. *Tailor's pressing iron made in the mid-19th century by Savery in Philadelphia, Pennsylvania. The handle of the iron was cast to the bottom after being shaped and twisted. (Kauffman Collection)*

foundry of Wood and Perot, who had an agency in New Orleans operating under the name of Wood and Miltenberger.

A combination of influences has caused a revival of interest in the cast iron objects of a century ago. The exodus of great numbers of city dwellers to the country has created a new demand for usable objects such as lamp posts, lawn furniture, shoe scrapers, shelf brackets, and many other similar objects. Most of these furnishings are attractive and useful when employed for their designed purpose; however, the practice of adapting lamp holders to containers for planting ivy is perhaps regrettable.

The exodus to the country has also created a great interest in the use and decoration of the open fireplace, and products of cast iron are well suited for both purposes. Objects such as trivets, gypsy kettles, waffle irons, and tea kettles are only a few of the ornaments which can be rightfully used on the hearth or the mantle over the fireplace. Mortars and pestles are very decorative on shelves, and a fluted biscuit dish can be used attractively as a wall hanging, particularly against aged wood such as pine or poplar.

Although the origin and use of some old objects are not known today, they should not be discarded, for research work is constantly bringing to light new data. Finally, the variety of uses of cast iron is evidence of the development of style and function in America, and these relics of the past will always be treasured by people who are collectors of Americana.

BIBLIOGRAPHY

MERCER, HENRY C. *The Bible in Iron.* Doylestown: The Bucks County Historical Society, 1941.

SCHUBERT, H. R. *The History of the British Iron and Steel Industry from 450 B.C. to 1775 A.D.* London: Rutledge & Kegan Paul, 1957.

SIMPSON, BRUCE L. *Development of the Metal Casting Industry.* Chicago: American Foundreymen's Association, 1948.

Plate 56. *Cast iron rooster weather vane with sheet iron tail, originally convered with gilt and red paint. (Courtesy of the New York State Historical Association, Cooperstown, New York)*

Plate 57, upper left. *Waffle iron with Pennsylvania folk art motifs. Similar designs were used on fractur and barn decorations. (Kauffman Collection)* Plate 58 and 61, at center. *Waffle iron made by S. Cook at Chatham, Connecticut. Extremely few waffle irons were signed by their makers. (Kauffman Collection)*

Plate 60, below. *One of a set of four iron armchairs cast at the Wood Foundry in Philadelphia in 1804. Another of the set is illustrated in* Horner's Blue Book of .Philadelphia Furniture, *plate 431. Each chair is marked "Robert Wood, Quaker Ridge Road, Philadelphia." The scrolls are very similar in form to those used on earlier objects made of wrought iron. The modified cabriole legs terminate in feet that suggest the style of Queen Anne. (Courtesy Israel Sack, Inc.)*

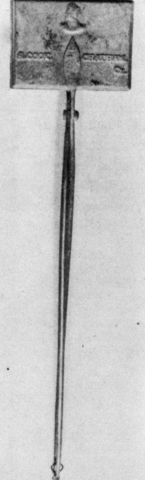

Plate 59, *above.* Hat tree and umbrella stand of cast iron, c.1850, believed to have been a personal possession of Washington Irving. Note the rococo detail in the base and the stylized floral design above. *(Courtesy Sleepy Hollow Restorations)*

50

CHAPTER FOUR

# The Blacksmith

THE BLACKSMITH WAS, WITHOUT a doubt, one of the first and most important craftsmen in the embryo industry of America, for James Read, blacksmith, came to Virginia with the Jamestown colonists in May, 1607; and in the very next year arrived another blacksmith, Richard Cole. The importance of the blacksmith in early America is further demonstrated by the inclusion of four additional smiths among a shipload of badly needed mechanics sent out to Virginia by the Virginia Company of London in 1611.

His importance in New England is emphasized by the following statement from the town records (1711) of Derby, Connecticut:

Voted that the town grant John Smith of Milford, blacksmith, four acres of land for a home lot, to build upon, anywhere within one mile of the meeting house where he shall choose, in land not laid out, upon condition that he build a mansion house and smith's shop, and set up the trade of a blacksmith, and follow it for the benefit of the inhabitants for the space of seven years.

Their importance is also underscored by the fact that they greatly outnumbered other craftsmen in metals throughout the eighteenth and nineteenth centuries. A business Directory of Boston for the year 1789 lists the following metal trades and the number of men engaged in each: coppersmiths 2, braziers 3, founders 5, farriers 7, silversmiths 2, tinplate workers 7, pewterers 4. But blacksmiths reached a total of 25. The *New Trade Directory of Philadelphia for 1800* reports about the same ratio of men engaged in the metal trades at about the same time; however, there was an addition of 22 whitesmiths working there. A study made by Shirley Martin in 1956 of metal craftsmen working in Bucks County, Pennsylvania, between 1750 and 1800 reports the following listing: Brass-founder 1, nailers 4, edge-tool maker 1, tinsmith 1, wheelwrights 34, blacksmiths 104. This report focuses attention on the fact that the distribution of metal craftsmen in a rural area was different from the pattern reported for city craftsmen.

Despite the fact that there were so many

51

Plate 62. *The initials of this primitive but important weather vane stand for William Penn, Samuel Carpenter, and Caleb Pusey. Few artifacts of such quality and importance have survived. (Courtesy of The Historical Society of Pennsylvania)*

blacksmiths in the early years of America, little is known about their personalities or their products, and notwithstanding the growing interest in tools and other objects made of iron, little research has been directed toward the subject. Researchers' apathy toward the smith could be attributed to the facts that there were so many of them, that their products have saturated the marketplace, that objects made of iron are often without aesthetic appeal, and that the functional quality of such implements and vessels reduces their appeal to a more glamorous-minded collecting fraternity. Yet most of these objections are overruled by the Collector's delight in "primitive" antiques, by the recent rise to importance of living museums, such as those at Sturbridge, Massachusetts; Shelburne, Vermont; and Old Salem, North Carolina; and by an obvious spurt of interest in the early technology of America.

Possibly the most valid explanation of the lack of interest in the blacksmith's products is that, since few of them were marked with his name, both the objects and their makers have fallen into obscurity. The most unfortunate result of this absence of identifying marks is that a collector cannot distinguish between imported objects and those made in America. Consequently, the collecting of objects made of iron often lacks the patriotic interest factor usually present when collecting objects made of pewter or silver.

Nevertheless, the impulse to assemble and preserve all sorts of Americana has quickened so much in recent years that the need for research on the blacksmith has become imperative. The finding of some marked pieces of iron, combined with data brought to light for the first time, will assist in placing them in a more favored position among craftsmen who worked in metal.

Plate 63. *Newspaper advertisement of Joseph Hammond that appeared in the New Hampshire Gazette, July 17, 1767. The range of work that he advertises focuses attention on the wide knowledge and versatile craftsmanship required of a blacksmith in the 18th century.*

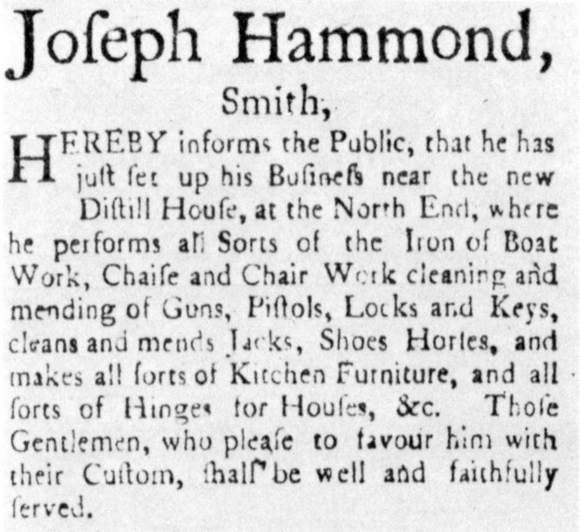

## Joseph Hammond,
### Smith,

HEREBY informs the Public, that he has juſt ſet up his Buſineſs near the new Diſtill Houſe, at the North End, where he performs all Sorts of the Iron of Boat Work, Chaiſe and Chair Work cleaning and mending of Guns, Piſtols, Locks and Keys, cleans and mends Jacks, Shoes Horſes, and makes all ſorts of Kitchen Furniture, and all ſorts of Hinges for Houſes, &c. Thoſe Gentlemen, who pleaſe to favour him with their Cuſtom, ſhall be well and faithfully ſerved.

The *Oxford English Dictionary*, Oxford, 1833, describes a blacksmith as, "A smith who works in iron or black metal, as distinguished from a 'whitesmith,' who works in tin or white metal." A more detailed description of the work done by the smith is found in *The Parents' and Guardians' Directory and Youth's Guide in the Choice of a Profession or Trade:*

This artificer makes the iron-work used about buildings and the coarser parts of kitchen furniture, as pokers, trevets, etc. He also mends utensils as happen to be broken. The blacksmiths now give themselves the general name of Smiths; theirs is a laborious business, which chiefly consists in the management of the fire, the hammer, and the file.

Another definition found in the *Mechanic's Companion,* by John Lochen, published in Philadelphia in 1845, tells that, "Smithing is the art of uniting several lumps of iron into one mass, and of forging any lump or mass of iron into an intended shape."

The tools of the blacksmith varied from time to time and from place to place. They

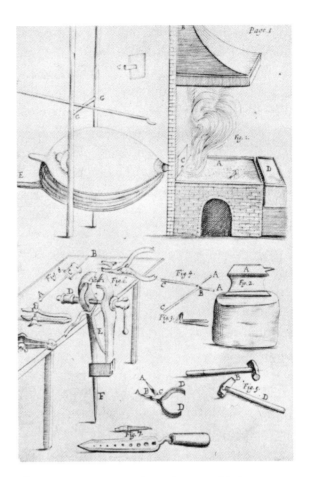

Plate 65. *Interior view of a 16th century blacksmith shop with forge, bellows and tools. Note the short horn on the anvil and the leg vise fastened to the bench and reaching to the floor. This illustration is from* Mechanick Exercises, *Moxon, London, 1703.*

Plate 64. *Interior of a blacksmith shop of the 19th century reconstructed and equipped for the "New Jersey Iron, 1674-1850" exhibit at the New Jersey State Museum at Trenton, New Jersey. Products made by the blacksmith as well as his tools are shown. Among the tools are two farrier's hammers, four nail headers, a hoof rest with a sole knife, a wheelwright's stand, and a flywhisk. (Courtesy of New Jersey State Museum)*

Plate 66. *Flatiron wrought by a blacksmith. The handle is forge welded to the base in the front and does not quite touch the iron at the rear. (Kauffman collection)*

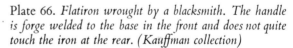

were generally divided into three groups. The first is the hearth with its bellows, water trough, shovels, tongs, rake, poker, and a water container for damping down the fire and cooking objects. The second group consists of the anvil, sledges, tongs, swages, cutters, chisels, and hammers. The third group was made up of the shoeing box which contains knives, rasps and files for preparing the horse's hooves for shoes, an iron stand for supporting the horse's foot while working on it, and a special hammer and nails to fasten the shoe to the hoof. If the smith were engaged in special types of work such as wheel or ship work, he needed tools designed for such work in addition to those enumerated above.

A boy became skilled in the use of the tools through a training procedure called apprenticeship. The European plan of apprenticeship had been transplanted to America, the prospective craftsman usually serving seven to nine years before his twenty-first birthday. If he were apprenticed to his father (as was often customary in the eighteenth century), he lived at home while he learned his trade, and here was taught the rudiments of reading, writing, and arithmetic. Keeping accounts and instruction in religious matters were sometimes included. This procedure kept the business in the family, for frequently the son worked until the father retired, and thus the family ownership of many businesses was continued through many generations. If he were apprenticed outside the home, he lived with his master, who was responsible for providing the same training the father gave his son. The following advertisement from the *Pennsylvania Packet and*

*Daily Advertiser,* August 1, 1789, describes the procedures governing apprenticeship training in Philadelphia at that time:

DELAWARE WORKS

Wanted at said works: Apprentices from ten to fourteen years of age, to learn the Nailing and Smith's business. The boys will be placed under the direction of sober, industrious workmen, and will be suitably cloathed and fed during their apprenticeship; and instructed in reading, writing, and arithmetic; and when of age will each receive one new suit of cloaths, and fifteen dollars in money, for the purpose of furnishing themselves with a set of tools.

The journeyman blacksmith to whom a boy was apprenticed managed all the details of the business. All apprentice contracts were very specific in forbidding the apprentice from transacting business on his master's property.

Before a discussion of the trade techniques of the early blacksmiths, the reader's attention should be directed to the fact that "how to do it" books from the eighteenth and early nineteenth centuries are almost nonexistent. The so-called "secrets of the trade" were passed by word of mouth from the master to the apprentice, and great care was taken to prevent them from falling into the possession of unauthorized persons.

A startling exception to this general rule is the book, *Mechanick Exercises or the Doctrine of Handy Works,* by Joseph Moxon, London, 1703. In addition to smithing, Moxon gives instruction in the arts of joinery, carpentry, turning, and bricklaying. The information in this book is obviously based on practices of the seventeenth century; however, no one who has written since that time about the subject of iron has failed to rely heavily on its contents.

Although Moxon discussed techniques in considerable detail, he does not preface his discussion with a description of the medium with which the blacksmith worked, as will be done now. The blacksmith worked with charcoal iron, so named because charcoal was used for fuel in the furnace that produced the iron. It seems not only to have been suited to the various ways it had to be "worked"; but because of its other desirable qualities, much of it has outlived iron of a later period which lacked these qualities.

It should also be noted that all charcoal iron was not of the same quality. The factors determining the quality seem to have been the quality of the ore which was mined, or dug, and the skill with which the iron was extracted from the ore. There was always considerable enthusiasm for iron that was produced in the region in which it was used; however, all users seem to have agreed that the best iron in the world was made in Sweden.

The following excerpt is taken from the *Diary of Matthew Patten of Bedford, New Hampshire, 1754-1788.* He reports on January 20, 1783 as follows:

I took a part of a Bar of Forge Iron to Mr. Shedes of 33 pounds for which he is to let me have Spanish or Swedes iron to make a chain for logging, and he laid an axe for me. The steel was mine and I gave him a half dollar in money.

Patten's limited use of the English language does not permit an accurate analysis to be made of his transaction; one can conclude, however, that he traded some domestic iron for a superior chain iron made abroad.

Moxon's appraisal of the quality of iron produced in different countries is as follows:

In most parts of England, we have an abundance of these iron-stones; but our English iron is generally a course sort of iron, hard and brittle, fit for Fire-bars, and other course uses; Unless it be about the Forrest of Dean, and some few places more, where the iron proves very good.

Swedish Iron is of all sorts, the best we use in England. It is a fine tough sort of iron, which will best endure the hammer, and is softest to the file; and therefore most coveted by Workmen to work upon.

Spanish Iron would be as good as Swedish iron, were it not subject to Red-sear, (As workmen call it) that is to crack between hot and cold. Therefore when it falls under your hand you must tend it more earnestly at the forge.

There is some iron comes from Holland (tho in no great quantity) but is made in Germany. This iron is called Dort Squares, only because it comes to us thence, and is wrought into square bars three quarters of an inch square. It is a bad course iron and only fit for slight uses, as Window bars, Brewers Bars, Fire Bars, etc.

These comments indicate that different qualities of iron were available to the blacksmiths of the seventeenth, eighteenth, and nineteenth centuries. It might be pointed out that even if a high grade of iron were used, the metal frequently needed additional attention by the smith before he used it. The limitations of the refining and rolling processes caused much of the iron to have an imperfect texture, usually referred to as fibrous. The blacksmith could improve this condition by heating the iron and vigorously hammering it on his anvil. This procedure assisted in removing certain impurities (which partially accounted for the fibrous texture) from the iron and improved its purity and resistance to disintegration. Despite the work which most smiths performed on the iron, it is not uncommon to find separations or fissures in objects such as axes, wheel tires, and fence parts.

Plate 67. *Typical great door hinge, used widely in New England for doors in churches and public buildings. This style gave better support than an ordinary strap hinge. The two parts were made by drawing out and reducing bars of iron to the desired shape and size. Surface irregularities are genuine outgrowth of hammering. Holes, obviously, were punched. (Courtesy Stamford Museum and Nature Center)*

## TRADE TECHNIQUES

A certain amount of improvement in the texture of the iron was inevitable since the blacksmith, after taking the iron of his rack, usually found it necessary to reshape it for his specific need. This was particularly true in the operation most frequently performed by the blacksmith, drawing out. This process was accomplished by heating the iron bar, laying it on the anvil, and increasing its length, or width, by using a cross-pein hammer, at the same time decreasing its other dimension, as necessary.

Plate 68. *Forged iron dough scraper with engraved initials "G.K." and decoration. The fissures and imperfections of hand wrought iron are very evident in this object of the early 18th century. (Courtesy of The Metropolitan Museum of Art, Gift of Mrs. J. Insley Blair, 1937)*

Drawing out not only improved the quality of the iron but its appearance as well. Certain irregularities in the surface (not pock marks) and cross-sectional variations in size are usually considered evidence of hand fabrication. Such variations can be observed only by close examination. They are the underlying reason for the charm of the handmade when compared with the mechanical perfection of metal sheet or strip which was made by a machine.

The virtues of "drawn out" work can be most easily seen in the scrolls of brackets, screens, baluster, or fences. After the bar was

Plate 69. *Shoe scraper at the front door of Carpenters Hall in Philadelphia, Pennsylvania. This piece incorporates the finest in design and workmanship to be found in wrought iron work. (Kauffman photo)*

Plate 70. *Typical baluster of the 19th century made from machine-fabricated band iron. The uniform thickness and width of the metal lacks the charm found in earlier hand-wrought pieces. (Kauffman photo)*

drawn out, and thinned toward the end of the bar, the craftsman started forming the scroll. The thin end of the bar was carefully formed on the horn of the anvil; and by continued heating and bending the iron, a scroll of any size and shape could be made without the use of a template or auxiliary device. If duplicates were needed, the smith frequently checked his form against a chalk line on the floor or on a large metal plate, but the operation was gauged by the hand and the eye rather than with calipers and scales. Other scrolls such as the bolt-end, leaf-end, half-penny, fish-tail, and snub-end required more skill and time, but they were shaped in the same general manner.

Another fundamental operation of the blacksmith was welding on the forge. Moxon describes the heats, three in number, that were necessary to the proper performance of the work. The hottest is *snowball* heat, which refers to white heat; this is used to weld iron. There is *full-welding heat,* not quite as hot as snowball, employed to weld

Plates 71-72. *The Reed house in New Castle, Delaware, has attractive ironwork in the first floor baluster and the second floor balcony. The view shows the fine bolt-end finials in the scrolls of the balusters. (Kauffman photos)*

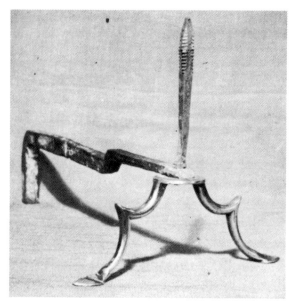

mild steel. The last is low or *light-welding heat,* rarely used because of the great skill required in using it.

Welding was often preceded by scarfing, which means tapering the ends or edges of parts before welding. Such tapered parts

were then reheated, and the ends overlapped the entire distance of the tapered parts. They were placed on the anvil and tapped until the two pieces were perfectly welded into one piece. If the joint were oversize, it was reheated and forged until all parts were of uniform thickness. This operation was performed on wheel tires, but the joint can rarely be found. Some blacksmiths used sand, as a flux, to keep the surface of the metal clean in the fire, but a good craftsman could work without this assistance.

An example of this lapping and welding technique is frequently found on andirons; after the bar supporting the wood was burned off from long normal use, the smith welded a new section of iron to the old, rather than make a whole new part. It is not uncommon to be able to detect the location

Plate 74. *The hooks on the back of this andiron were attached by forge welding. It was difficult to weld a small piece of iron to a large piece, as was done in this example. The large ball at the top was made by upsetting. (Courtesy of The Stamford Museum and Nature Center)*

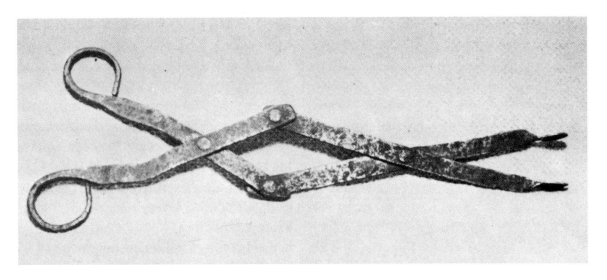

Plate 75. *Tongs for lifting hot coals from the fire. Although the form and workmanship are not very refined, the tongs seem to function very efficiently. All joints are riveted. (Kauffman Collection)*

of the lap weld on such a repair. This type of repair does not guarantee that the object is very old, but it is proof that the repair was made on the forge and not with a welding torch.

Upsetting was the opposite of drawing out, for in this operation the length of the bar was decreased instead of increased. A portion of the bar was heated to welding heat and other parts cooled so that when the end of the bar was hammered the hot portion was made thicker and the total length of the bar was decreased. The enlarged portion was then finished with a hammer, or with swages, if a design with some specific details was desired.

Punching was quite simple but very important for decorative purposes and for joining pieces of iron. It was the only method known by which a hole one inch in diameter could be made in a bar one-inch wide. The first operation was to heat the bar and slightly increase its width by upsetting. Then, after reheating, a small punch was forced through the hot part of the bar with a hammer, until the punch was stopped by the face of the anvil. The punch was pulled out of the bar, the bar reheated, and punched from the opposite side until there was a small hole through the bar. The bar was reheated the third time and the hole placed over an opening in the anvil, where it was stretched to the desired diameter with larger punches. Such holes usually have a burr on the bottom side, and the bar was always wider at the hole than at any other part. At times, the enlarged portion was utilized to form part of the design of an object. Its use, like the other techniques described, does not guarantee great age, but it does indicate that it was hand-wrought.

Various methods were used by blacksmiths to join pieces of iron: riveting, collaring, pinning, screwing, and bolting. Rivets had round or countersunk heads. When a countersunk-head was used, the head and the riveted end were flush with the surface of the iron, making them difficult to detect if the ironwork is heavily painted. When rivets with round heads were used, the portion hammered over, or riveted was the same size and shape as the original head. Collaring was done by wrapping a band of iron around two pieces to join them together; scrolls were frequently fastened to bars, or to each other, by this plan. There were various ways of pinning pieces of iron together; the type most frequently used resembled a mortise and tennon joint, with the tennon going completely through the mortise and held in place with a tapered wedge or pin of iron. Such a joint was used on some early andirons. Screwing and bolting were used in the nineteenth century. Bolted joints are undesirable if the bolt is secured with a nut. An alternative was to tap a thread on one of the bolted parts and dispense with the nut.

Twisting was another technique widely used by craftsmen in iron. It was easily executed by heating the portion of the iron to be twisted to a blood-red heat; one end was then placed in a vise and the other end twisted with a holding device of some kind. The modern iron worker uses a monkey-wrench; the tool in its present form, however, was not available before the nineteenth century. The spirals could be made tight or loose and the direction of the twist could be reversed a number of times if the craftsman wished to do so. A very long twist required a number of "heats." Rarely has a craftsman had at his command such a simple but effective decorative technique.

Repoussé in iron was rarely used in America, but was widely used in Europe from the twelfth to the eighteenth century. The work required a high degree of skill and a complete understanding of the forms used. Popular designs were human figures, masks, flowers, and the acanthus leaf. The last-named was widely used as an embellishment on scrolls. Very poor duplicates of this form were made in America during the early part of the twentieth century revival of interest in objects made of wrought iron.

The best known master of repoussé was Jean Tijou, a famous French blacksmith, who did much of the ironwork for Hampton Court Palace and St. Paul's Cathedral. His work at Hampton Court was profuse with ornamentation, but at St. Paul's his designs were restrained by the cathedral's architect, Sir Christopher Wren.

Engraving was another popular decorating technique, but it was used principally by

Plate 76. *Cellar window grill on a house on Delancy Street, Philadelphia, Pennsylvania, containing repousse work rarely found in America. There is the possibility, of course, that this one was imported. (Kauffman photo)*

**EARLY AMERICAN IRONWARE ✦ 60**

foreign craftsmen. The pattern was cut by removing small threads of iron with a pointed tool, usually called a graver. Some engraving was done on American door and gun locks made of iron.

The finishing of iron work holds much interest for connoisseurs who try to separate the new from the old. Novices assume that the pock-marked texture often found on modern reproductions is evidence of hand production. No fact could be more distant from the truth, for there is evidence gathered from a study of the tools and techniques used by craftsmen, that they tried to make the surface of the metal as smooth as possible. As a matter of fact, there was a tool called a flatter, which was used to make the iron flat after it was "drawn-out." A careful examination of surviving old objects of iron reveals surfaces so smooth that it is almost impossible to detect hammer marks on them.

Edges and bevels were often smoothed with a file; and there is evidence of competence in the using of files when they were crudely made in comparison to the quality that is available today. It should be noted that file marks were virtually never left on objects; they are usually evidence of indifferent workmanship. Powered abrasives were available in early times; and in the eighteenth century, paper coated with abrasives came into use.

## PRODUCTS OF THE BLACKSMITH

Perhaps the question most difficult to answer in the research on the trade of the blacksmith is: What did he make? It is evident that the answer varies, for it is dependent on the place and time that he worked. For example, the work of a blacksmith who lived in an agricultural community in the early eighteenth century would differ a great deal from the work of one who lived in a seaport early in the nineteenth century. Their shops and equipment were similar, but one made and "mended" ploughs while the other made and "mended" objects which were used on a ship.

Plate 78. *Iron trivet having legs attached with functional, unobtrusive rivets. (Kauffman Collection)*

Perhaps the most striking observation to be made of the trade is the surprisingly infrequent entries of horse-shoeing found in the ledgers of men who worked in the eighteenth century. This curious situation can be explained by the fact that there were few hard surface roads at that time and shoeing was not necessary. It is evident that the anatomy of the horse was designed to perform without shoes and it was his travel on hard roads that required him to be shod. It should also be pointed out that there was a craftsman called a farrier, whose major concern was shoeing and caring for the health of horses, and thus the blacksmith devoted much of his time to making and repairing other objects of iron.

Research indicates that there was a constantly changing pattern of work for the blacksmiths of the eighteenth and nineteenth centuries. Examination of the daybook of John Miller, a blacksmith in Lancaster, Pennsylvania, from 1744 to 1764,

and of another kept by James Anderson of Williamsburg, Virginia, reveals the types of work which these men performed in their shops in the mid-eighteenth century. Newspaper advertisements add still more to our knowledge, but they rarely tell completely what a smith did. The following hypothesis seems to emerge from the facts at hand.

It seems evident that many of the blacksmiths of the eighteenth and nineteenth centuries were engaged in making a large variety of small objects; but rarely made sets of tools or house hardware. In addition, they also did a great deal of repair and replacement work; so these craftsmen might be logically called "general blacksmiths." Sample entries in their daybooks are as follows:

...to altering 56 harrow teeth, to mending a pair of stillards, to plating a large plough, to mending a bridle bar and a hook, to repairing a loop for a beam, to dress a coulter, to repairing and axe, to 3 iron rim door locks, to two pairs of H hinges, to welding a

Plate 79. *Unusually fine pair of andirons with spit hooks on the front of the columns, and finals on the top of the columns formed by a technique known as "upsetting". Probably of the late 18th century. (Courtesy of the Metropolitan Museum of Art, The Sylmaris Collection, Gift of George Coe Graves, 1930)*

Plate 80. *Colonial American kitchen, reproduced at the New Jersey State Museum, Trenton, New Jersey, as part of the "New Jersey Iron, 1674–1850" exhibition held during the summer of 1954. (Courtesy of the New Jersey State Museum)*

chain, to plating the bar for a plough, to mending a padlock, to 2 staples, to shoeing two horses round, to laying a large poll axe, to pointing a plough, to a poaker, to 8 hoops for buckets, to a pot rack, to a boe for a key, and a door mat for Sally's room.

Most general blacksmiths probably made objects for the hearth.

These objects include cranes, and irons, trammels, tongs, shovels, trivets, small game spits, skillets, toasters, skewer holders, etc. It should also be noted that although these objects were primarily of a functional nature, many of them were simply and beautifully decorated by the blacksmith.

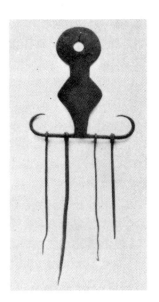

Plate 81. *Iron skewers and holder, propably very common in the 18th century but now very rare. (Courtesy of The Metropolitan Museum of Art, Gift of Alice Porter, 1927)*

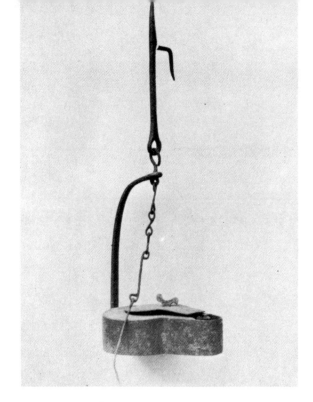

Plate 82. *Because Betty lamps were often finished in bright metal they are usually considered to be the product of the whitesmith. However some were left black and were produced by blacksmiths, such as this example from Pennsylvania, made, probably, about the middle of the 18th century. Its height is 11¼ inches and its breadth, 4¼ inches. (Courtesy of The Metropolitan Museum of Art, Gift of Mrs. Robert W. de Forest, 1933)*

The most frequently needed object for the fireplace is a set of andirons. These are usually made up of three major parts; a horizontal bar on which the logs were placed to facilitate burning, a short back leg to raise the bar from the heart, and a tall front column, strap, or shaft, which supported the front end of the horizontal bar and prevented the logs from rolling off the bar on the hearth. The height of the front column varies according to the size of the opening in the fire place, however, their usual height range is from fifteen to thirty inches. The tall andirons used in kitchen fireplaces often had hooks attached on the front or back of the tall iron column to support a roasting spit. The hooks were called spithooks. Short andirons with round or faceted finials were made for small fireplaces in the bedrooms.

Most kitchen fireplaces had a fitting called a crane, or a sway. This also had three major parts. A vertical bar was installed in two screw eyes in a back corner of the fireplace. To this was attached a horizontal bar with a hook on the opposite end. This bar could sway over the fire for cooking and then forward so that the pots could be removed or emptied. The third part was a diagonal brace to support the horizontal bar. This bar was often twisted to make it decorative as well as functional. Pothooks, called trammels, were also suspended from the horizontal bar to hold the various pots and kettles in which food was prepared over the fire.

Trivets were usually round, triangular, square, or shaped like a heart. They usually had three short legs, an inch or two long, and some had handles cleverly forged as an integral part of a leg. Their function was to keep a kettle in the simmering stage over some coals on the floor of the hearth.

Spits had a number of hooks mounted on them to support small game or birds as they were roasted before the fire. Toasters had a base and a rack that rotated so that slices of bread could be toasted on both sides without removing them from the toaster.

The skewer holder with its skewers is the rarest fireplace fitting today. These diminutive objects were indispensable in attaching a roast to a spit, but have only a decorative function today. Only a few sets have come

**EARLY AMERICAN IRONWARE ✦ 64**

upon the market in recent years and there are hundreds of buyers for each set available. It should be noted that some reproductions have been made that bear a marked similarity to the originals.

Many lighting fixtures were made by the blacksmith, and of particular importance is the American floor candlestand. They usually have three legs, forged into attractive tapering bows, and joined to form a support for a single vertical rod. A horizontal and adjustable yoke, or cross-support slides on the vertical rod, and holds two brass cups for candles. Beneath the cups are drip-dishes to prevent the melted wax from dropping on the floor. These floor candlestands are a rare and costly form of American ironwork.

Some signed Betty lamps can be identified as products of American blacksmiths, although many of these lamps were probably

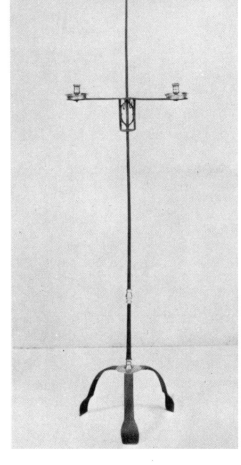

Plate 83. *Rare iron and brass candlestand with original brass cups, finial, and iron snuffers, 65½ inches high and 20½ inches wide, c.1720–1740, an heirloom of the family of Captain Daniels of Nantucket. (Courtesy of Israel Sack, Inc.)*

made in Birmingham, England and imported by American merchants. They were more noted for their smoke than their light; however, they are important objects of iron, and no colonial setting seems complete without one.

In addition to these household objects made of iron by the blacksmith, there is

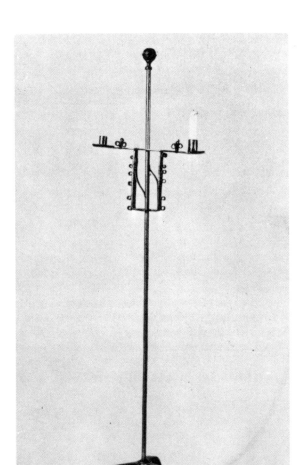

Plate 84. *Two-armed candlestand of Pennsylvania origin. Stands utilizing both brass and iron are rare and this example probably is unique. An unknown maker's initials are stamped on its "penny" feet. (Courtesy of the Philadelphia Museum of Art)*

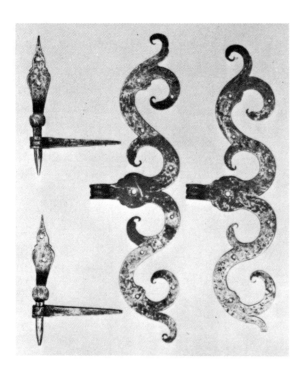

Plate 85. *Pair of Pennsylvania staghorn hinges with pintles. The horizontal spikes of the pintles were driven into the wood of the door frame instead of being fastened on it, as might be assumed from this photo. (Courtesy of The Metropolitan Museum of Art, Gift of Mrs. J. Insley Blair, 1949)*

another class of products generally known as architectural hardware. One of the earliest, the most widely known and the most attractive of these objects, was the long strap hinge. These were mounted horizontally on doors made of vertical boarding and on later doors which were joined at the corners with a mortise and tenon joint. The hinge was usually nailed to the door; however, it is possible that screws were used in some cases. One end of the hinge projected beyond the back edge of the door and fitted over a vertical stud (driven into the door frame) called a pintle. The hinge usually tapered in width from the hinge joint to the other end where it terminated in a form such as a tulip or a heart. The surface of the hinge was usually beveled along the edge, and sometimes the edges were ornamented by forging half-round lobes or spurs beyond the main body of the hinge. Although the cast iron butt hinge was invented in England in 1775, it is evident that long strap hinges were used in America for at least another century. A plain manufactured variety was used on large barn doors in the early twentieth century.

FOR SALE BY

*Isaac Hazlehurst & Co.*

A GENERAL Assortment of India Goods
Hyson and singlo teas
China ware
Silks, and sewing silks
(Imported directly from India and China)
Madeira wine, old and fit for immediate use
Ditto of different quality and age
Teneriffe wine
Claret of superior quality
Inferior ditto
French white wine vinegar in barrels and kegs
Dutch brass kettles
German patent medicines
German bibles, prayer books, Arendt's Christenthum and school books
Newemberg toys for children
German scythes 9 and 10 hands, and whetstones
Dutch Rappee snuff
Horn lanthorn leaves
Glass pint cannisters, with screw stoppers
Black and Seneca snake root
A few tons of logwood
Bourdeaux rough hewn building stone
Virginia coal

*And the following Articles Manufactured at*

Delaware Works:

Nails, 3d, 4d, 8d. 10d, 12d & 20 flat & sharp points
Deck, drawing and sheathing nails
Pump and scupper nails
Flooring brads, 12d and 20d
Shovels
American steel faggoted
Nail rods of different sizes

W A N T E D,

A Person who understands the making of H and HL hinges; and also a Locksmith—Good Encouragement will be given by applying as above, or to *Samuel Ogden*, at the Works. *Dec2 9* w&ttf

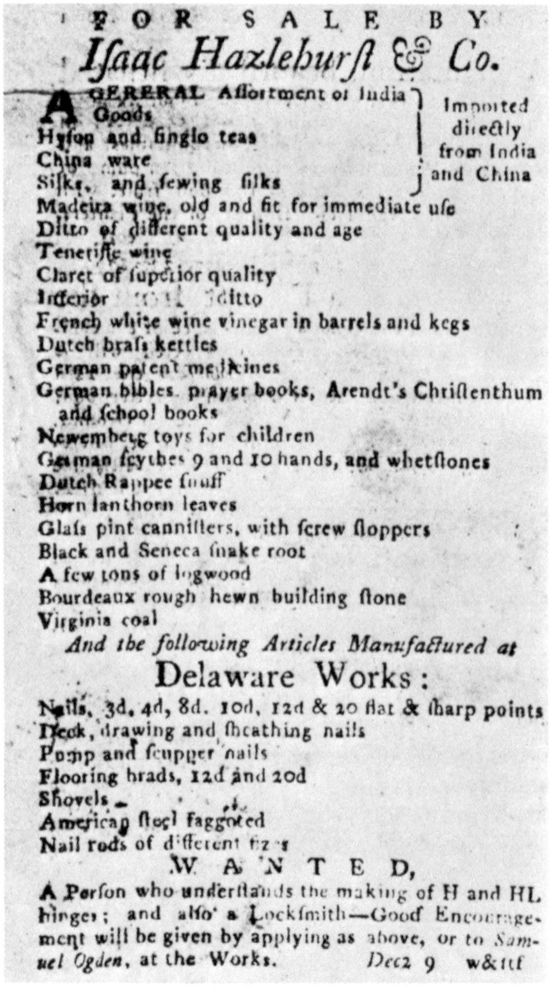

Plate 86. *Interesting advertisement from the Pennsylvanvı Packet and Daily Advertiser of December 2, 1789. It enumerates a number of items imported by merchant Hazlehurst and also gives some interesting details of American-produced wares. The making of H and HL hinges is particularly interesting. (Courtesy of the Historical Society of Pennsylvania)*

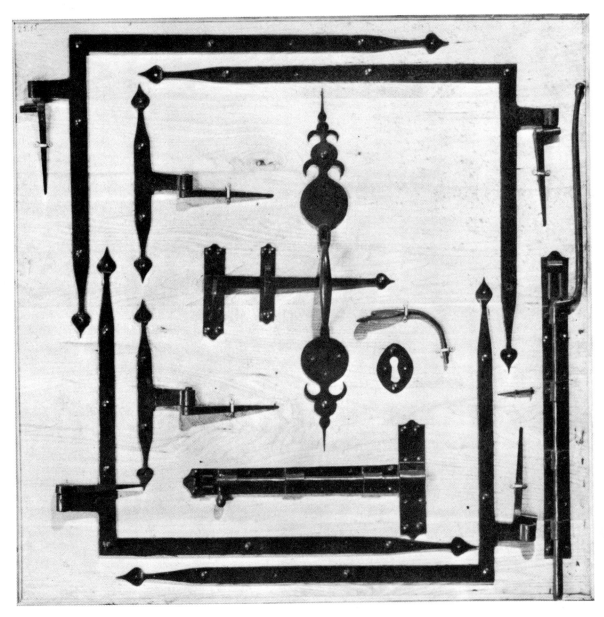

Plate 87. *Twelve pieces of hardware from the doors of St. Stephens Church, East Haddam, Connecticut. The museum accession card indicates they were made by a family of blacksmiths named Warner, presumably local craftsmen. The large and complete Suffolk latch, mounted in the middle of the panel, is an elegant example of New England workmanship. (Courtesy of the Wadsworth Atheneum, Hartford)*

Another type of hinge using a pintle is known as a "staghorn" hinge in America. The style seems to be a scaled-down version of similar large hinges used on early cathe-drals and castles in Europe. The name is derived from their form which frequently resembles the intricate arrangement of horns on the head of a deer. They were usually

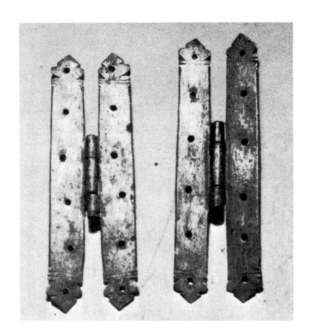

Plate 88. *Pair of H hinges having unusual foliated ends, with the design produced by filing, and the usual hammer marks removed from the surface by draw filing. (Kauffman Collection)*

forged from one piece of iron and required much skill and labor to fabricate. European examples, similar to those made in America, are usually very ornate and a few were covered with a thin coating of tin to protect the iron from the deteriorating effects of damp climates. Staghorn hinges were used principally in the Dutch and German settlements in America.

It is evident that there were occasions when a pintle could not be used as a second part of a strap hinge. A pintle required a heavy framework for mounting, such as was usually used in exterior walls for outside doors. Inside partitions were sometimes made of vertical boarding; and in such cases, the long strap was attached with a pin to another member which was mounted on a wall surface flush with the door. The shape of the second member varied. However, it

Plate 89. *Cupboard with strap hinges and a second member not a pintle, well suited to furniture rather than to large doors. (Himmelreich Collection)*

usually covered a wider area than the strap, and at times closely resembled the form of a staghorn hinge.

Large L-shaped hinges were used in New England throughout the eighteenth century. (Plate 21) They were used most frequently on large outside house or church doors and were hooked on pintles which were driven into the door frames in the traditional manner. Some smaller types of L hinges were attached to a second vertical member with a pin and were known as H and L hinges. When the horizontal part of the hinge was dropped, it was known as an H hinge. Most H hinges were small and were used on inside doors. There is documentary evidence that

Plate 90. *Unusual array of New England latches and hinges at Old Sturbridge Village. New England blacksmiths seem to have favored geometrically shaped finials on their Suffolk latches. Seven Norfolk latches are attached on the middle-right portion of the panel. (Courtesy of Old Sturbridge Village, Sturbridge, Massachusetts)*

H hinges were made in America; however, no criterion has been established to distinguish the indigenous from the foreign.

An endless variety of hinges were used on feed boxes, shutters, cupboards, chests, bible boxes, candle boxes, etc. Chest hinges are often "scaled-down" versions of door hinges and are often composed of two straps which are joined with a pin. Many fine hinges were used on the blanket chests made in Pennsylvania. The tulip was a favored motif on Pennsylvania chest hinges, and a few hinges are known to have repoussé work on them. Charcoal renderings of many fine hinges can be found in *Early American Wrought Iron* by Albert Sonn.

Although there is a lively interest among museums and collectors in all objects made

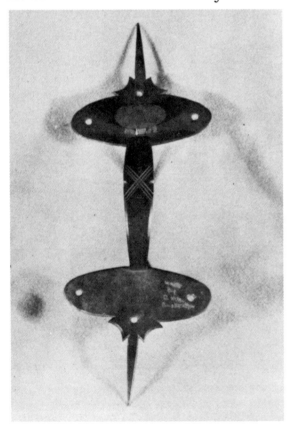

by the American blacksmith, such as locks, hinges, andirons, trivets, etc., the Suffolk hand latch is considered the real *piéce de résistance*. This latch was used on inside doors when no lock was required or on outside doors when, for the purpose of locking, a bar was used or a rim lock which lacked a latch facility. The over-all length of the latches varied from ten inches to approximately forty inches. The small sizes were used on common inside doors while the large types were utilized on church doors and those of other public buildings.

The latches were usually composed of five parts; (1) the handle, as a rule forged from one piece of iron, consisting of an upper and lower cusp with the hand grasp in between; (2) the thumb lift, consisting of a flat or curved plate on one end, the other end extending through the door to raise the bar and to provide a handle so that the door could be opened from either side; (3) the bar, a long piece of strap iron attached horizontally to the door, with one nail and held in place by a (4) staple; and (5) a catch, usually shaped like the number four with a long tapered point, which was driven into the door frame to secure the door.

The handle which appeared on the outside of the door was the critical part on which the blacksmith lavished his skill and ingenuity. It was usually forged of one piece of iron, although a type used at Farmington, Con-

Plate 91. *Suffolk latch marked "D. King" on the hand grip. Evidence indicates that D. King worked in the central Massachusetts area. The holes for mounting, originally punched, appear to have been rounded smooth with a modern drill or countersink. (Courtesy of the Wooster Museum of Art)*

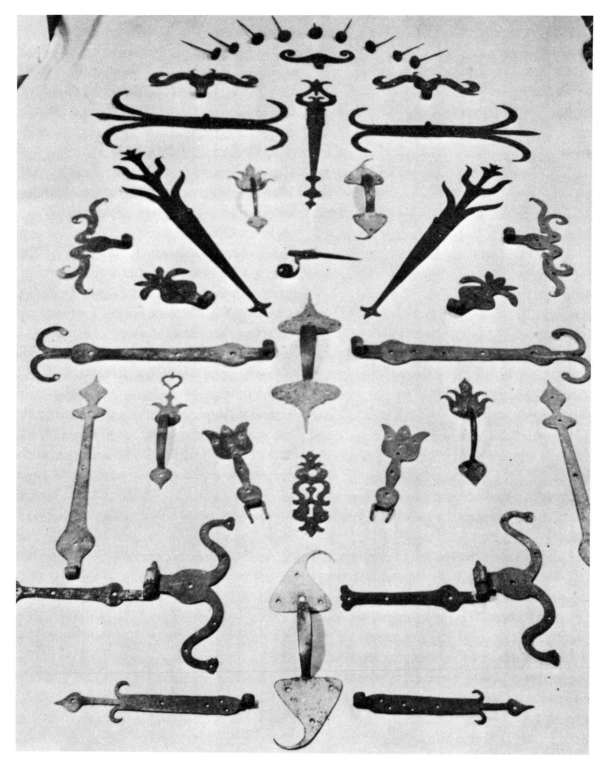

Plate 92. *Panel of iron objects most of which were made in Pennsylvania. The pair of hinges with tulip finials, placed diagonally near the top, are unique. The latch with the heart finial at left-center is also a very choice item. It has been sold and resold a number of times since the collection was dispersed. (Formerly the Himmelreich Collection)*

**71 ✦ THE BLACKSMITH**

necticut, was made up of separate cusps and a handle. The top cusp was generally the larger of the two and the bottom cusp was an inverted copy of the top. However, some latches lacked a bottom cusp; and in these cases, the bottom end of the handle was driven throughout the door and clenched on the other side. Cusp designs varied from place to place; however, the simulated lima bean was used over a long span of years and in most of the places where latches were used in America. The bean latches usually had flat strap handles, which were widest in the center and tapered toward the ends. They were usually of the small type and rarely had any ornamentation.

The thumb lift on the outside of the door was either a flat or curved plate; sometimes it was attached to the handle with a pin and was called a swivel-lift. Other latch handles had only a hole punched in the upper cusp through which the lift projected to the inner side of the door. On these latches the lift was enlarged in back of the plate by partially "slitting off" a tongue, which held the lift in place.

Although the function of the latch handle was obviously of first importance, its ornamentation determined its charm. The handle, usually semicircular in shape, was frequently ornamented by filling designs on the outer flat surface, or by swaging the center portion of a round handle to enlarge and ornament it. Sonn shows very few of the second type. Many collectors regard the second type as European; however, there is little, if any, documentation to support this hypothesis.

In the contour of the cusps we find an endless variety of designs, many of which defy classification. However, certain patterns were in common usage in the various parts of America throughout the eighteenth and nineteenth centuries. The arrowhead, the swordfish, the ball and spear, and the tulip design were popular in New England. Craftsmen in Pennsylvania seem to have been partial to motifs such as hearts, tulips, birds, cocks, etc. Some geometric designs were used in Pennsylvania, but they were usually less attractive than those derived from nature.

The parts of the latches located on the inside of the door were more important for their function than for their decorative quality. The style showed little variation in the different areas where latches were used. The surface of the bar was enriched in some cases by filing designs on and curves were filed on the edges with a round, or half-round, file. Sometimes a knob was also attached to the bar. Some of the catches were highly ornamented by attaching on the front a support, which was twisted and nailed to the door frame below the catch. This support helped to keep the catch in a horizontal position, but its use was probably more decorative than functional.

It is evident from the style, method of manufacture, and examples found *in situ* that the Suffolk latch was a creation of the blacksmith of the eighteenth century. The design of the Norfolk latch differed from that of the Suffolk, but there is some evidence that an early, handmade type of the Norfolk latch was also used in the eighteenth century.

Contemporary records, style, and methods of manufacture indicate, however, that

  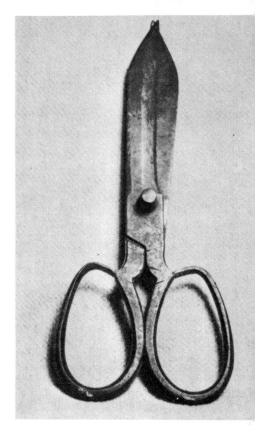

Plate 93. *The Norfolk thumb latch was widely used on the Atlantic seaboard. The uniform thickness of the back plate in this example suggest that it was made of rolled rather than forged metal. The handle probably was swaged in a die to form the attractive ornament in the center. (Kauffman Collection)* Plate 94. *This clamp, fastened on the edge of a table, was used for sewing and ripping. It has a distinct homemade quality. (Kauffman Collection)* Plate 95. *The widespread need for shears suggest that most blacksmiths had to be adept in making this popular household tool. (Kauffman Collection)*

the Norfolk latch was a favorite in the nineteenth century.

About the middle of the nineteenth century, the demand for cheap goods and the lack of interest in objects made by hand led to the production of complete latches made of cast iron. This type of mass production demanded that only a few designs could be utilized, and each latch was a perfect duplication of the pattern from which it was made. The wide usage of cheap mortise locks and the lack of interest in objects made by hand led to the demise of the Suffolk and Norfolk latches late in the nineteenth century.

It is also very important to note that throughout the eighteenth and nineteenth centuries, a spring latch was used, the mechanism of which was attached to a single plate, which was either square or shaped to resemble a keyhole in a horizontal position. The latch-bar was raised by turning a knob which was round or egg-shaped, and it fell into the catch by the action of a spring. A few of this type had a small night-latch that could be operated only on the inside of the door. There is no documentary evidence that this type was made in America; however, it is likely that some were made by blacksmiths working in those inland towns

Plate 96. *Iron three-legged pan with the marking "G.W. Ibach" on the handle. The shape of the vessel suggests production in the 18th century, but the style of lettering used in the name is typical of the 19th century. Ibach is a common name in Lancaster County, Pennsylvania, where a number of such vessels have been found bearing the name. Although this does not prove they were made there, it is quite likely that they were. (Kauffman Collection)*

not having easy access to imports in the cities of Boston, New York, Philadelphia, and Charleston.

The forms of these spring latches were quite standardized, and they lack the charm of the other handmade patterns; however, they were very efficient and widely used in America.

Although the names and the products of most of the general blacksmiths (and the specialists as well) will never be known, it is interesting to note that some data is available about a few. On July 6-13, 1732, William Bryant advertised his wares in the *Boston News-Letter,* indicating that he made and repaired many objects, including "housework":

Blacksmith.—This is to give notice, that there is one William Bryant, Blacksmith, that now keeps a shop adjoining the presbyterian Meeting House in Long Lane, Boston, who makes and mends Glaziers' vises, Cloathers' screws, and Worsted Combs, and makes, grinds, and sets Cloathers' Shears; he also makes and

mends Smiths' vises, Ship Carpenters' Blockmakers', Tanners', Glovers' and Coopers' Tools, Braziers' and Tinmens' Shears, and makes Housework, with many other things too tedious to mention. He will make and engage his work for any of his Employers' according to the value of them.

Unfortunately, none of Mr. Bryant's products has been identified nor has any of Mr. Lingard's, who advertised in the *South Carolina Gazette* (Charleston) on May 21, 1753. Mr. Lingard was more specific about the

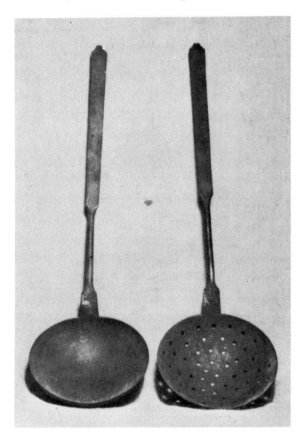

Plate 97. *Dippers and skimmers must have been a standard product of the Pennsylvania blacksmith. They were usually made in pairs, to which a fork, sometimes, was added. The handles frequently were decorated with incised designs. (Kauffman Collection)*

kind of decorative work he did; although, of course, most of his products fall into the category of general blacksmithing. His advertisement follows:

JAMES LINGARD, Smith and Farrier, makes all kinds of scroll work for grates and stair cases; ship, jack, and lock work, and all other kinds of smith's work at his shop on Mr. Maine's (commonly called Frankland or Sinclair's) wharf. Gentlemen that employ him, may depend on having their business done to satisfaction with all possible dispatch, and at the most reasonable rates. N.B.—He will take care of gentlemen's horses, and see that they have good care in case of sickness.

JAMES LINGARD

A final example of the combining of general products with decorative iron pieces is that of William Perkins of Philadelphia. His advertisement in the *Pennsylvania Journal* on April 23, 1785 mentions a variety of articles,

Plate 99. *Churchyard gate at Old Christ Church, Philadelphia, Pennsylvania. This is one of the few signed and dated pieces of its kind in America. It was made by Wheeler in 1785. (Kauffman photo)*

Plate 98. *Bolt-end scrolls in the iron gates at Old Christ Church, Second Street, Philadelphia, Pennsylvania. This type probably is the most attractive of all finials used on scroll work. (Kauffman photo)*

and interestingly, includes hinges for shutters and doors.

The problem of documenting objects of iron made in America has been solved only partially at this time. As the above-mentioned examples indicate, the names of some craftsmen are known but none of their products has ever been identified. This survey will also refer to objects imprinted with the names of the makers, about whom, unfortunately, nothing is known. Although these incomplete cases constitute a majority of those considered in this study, it is reported with a great deal of pride that a few of the problems are partially solved here.

If Philadelphia has supplied an interesting example of an ironworker whose art cannot

be identified today (Mr. Perkins), one of the most fully-solved cases also comes from this city. It has been generally known since the publication of *Early American Wrought Iron* by Sonn that the iron gate at Trinity Church on Second Street was made in 1785 by S. Wheeler. This data is placed on the gate and can be readily seen by anyone who examines it carefully; however, since virtually nothing was known about S. Wheeler, there was little interest in this information. Recently, however, the writer learned that one of the corner posts of a balcony on Congress Hall is inscribed with the name S. Wheeler.

This information sparked a renewed interest in this craftsman, with the result that a brief biography of him was found in *Lives of Eminent Philadelphians Now Deceased,* published by William Brotherhood in 1859. Here we learn that Samuel Wheeler was born in 1742 at Wicaco, an early Swedish settlement in South Philadelphia. He was an eminent ironworker in the city and was relieved of active military duty during a portion of the Revolution so that he could fabricate an iron chain, designed to impede the British from sailing up the Hudson River, a commission he was awarded because he was an excellent welder of iron. He is also credited with having designed an extraordinary cannon, which was captured by the British at the Battle of Brandywine, and is now displayed at the Tower of London.

He was a member and vestryman of the Swedish Wicaco Church (now Gloria Dei), and died May 10, 1820. It is interesting to note that Wheeler was inconspicuously listed as a blacksmith in the 1786 business directory for the city of Philadelphia.

In New York City an unsolved production mystery is the wrought iron balcony on Federal Hall. Federal Hall, formerly New York City's municipal building, was turned over to the national government and reconstructed from plans prepared by Major L'Enfant, the French engineer who laid out the city of Washington. On this balcony George Washington was inaugurated as the first President of the United States. The central motif of the ironwork consists of thirteen arrows, symbolic of the thirteen states. It is hardly conceivable that the commission for executing the ironwork for this famous site would have been given to anyone living outside the boundaries of the new nation. The New York City Hall records contain entries for the work done on the building in 1789; but there is no mention of the maker of the balcony, and today he remains unknown. The portion of the balcony with the arrows is now in the possession of the New York Historical Society.

The final examples to be documented in the field of decorative iron were made in Charleston, South Carolina, in the nineteenth century. There several attributions are made to Thibaut, and some positive recognition is given to Roh, Iusti, and Werner.

Jacob P. Roh was born in Wurtenburg, Germany, in 1776. He is first mentioned as a blacksmith in the city directory of Charleston in 1807, and he became a citizen on December 15, 1819. He was a member of St. John's Lutheran Church; and in January, 1822, was commissioned to make the fence and gates for the church.

Plates 100-2. *During the restoration of Congress Hall on Chestnut Street in Philadelphia in 1962 the paint was removed from the iron balcony and the name and date, "S. Wheeler, 1788" came to light, indicating that he had made this balcony as well as the gate of Old Christ Church, two of the most important objects made of iron in America. The engraving shows the balcony and Chestnut street as it appeared in 1800. (Courtesy National Park Service)*

**77  ✦  THE BLACKSMITH**

The gates were designed by A. P. Reeves. Mr. Roh employed eight men to do the job and received $2,735.13 for the work contracted by him. Alston Deas comments briefly on the gates in his book, *The Early Ironwork of Charleston,* introducing the subject with the words, "(the gate and fence are) beyond the scope of this volume, nevertheless a few words on the subject are appropriate."

A different point of view was taken by Samuel Lapham, Jr. and Albert Simons in an article in the *Architectural Forum,* dated January, 1924:

These gates were made by members of the congregation, among whom where the best wrought-iron craftsmen in the city, and were plainly a labor of love. Although less well-known, they are the equal of any of the other masterpieces of wrought-iron work of the city.

It seems strange that Deas could not extend the scope of his book to include one of the city's major works of art; although it certainly could not be called a product of the early period, it is unique and is an important part of this survey.

The handsome gates of St. Michael's Churchyard are Iusti's masterpiece. He also made a pavement grille which formerly was laid in front of a drug store in Meeting Street. The name of the proprietor is formed in wrought iron and the work is dated 1848. The means by which the grille was identified are not known; the overthrow of the gate, however, is signed in cast letters, "A. Iusti, Fecit, Charleston, S. C."

Another blacksmith of Charleston, Christopher Werner, is famous for his creation of iron, copper, and brass called the Palmetto Tree, on the grounds of the State House at Columbia, South Carolina. He also made the Sword Gate, with its high brick wall posts and octagonal lantern. The military accent of the gate suggests that it was designed for the Guardhouse; but because of a disagreement over the price, was never used for its original purpose.

Frederick Ortmann was the last blacksmith of Charleston to make gates and fences of wrought iron. In 1880 he made the gate located at 34 Broad Street in that city. His principal motif was a conventionalized lyre, the lyre being a Charleston favorite for at least one and one-half centuries.

It seems evident that the various gates, fences, balconies, etc., made by the American blacksmith are the most important of his products. Some of these objects are essential parts of historical shrines, and in a sense, are public property which should be preserved for posterity to study and admire. There are, however, less important objects which are excellent examples of American craftsmanship in iron which are available to museums and the collectors of Americana.

Attention will now be given to the men who did some "general blacksmithing" but might well be regarded as "specialists" in the making of objects of iron.

### BIBLIOGRAPHY
ANDERSON, JAMES. Manuscript daybook of James Anderson, blacksmith in Williamsburg, Virginia, last half eighteenth century.

CATALOGUE. *Early Arts of New Jersey, New Jersey Iron from 1674-1850.* An exhibition at the New Jersey State Museum, Trenton. May through October, 1954.

MARTIN, SHIRLEY. *Craftsmen Working in Metals in Bucks County, Pennsylvania, between 1750 and 1800.* Unpublished thesis at University of Delaware, 1956.

Plate 103. *Section of railing from Federal Hall in New York City where George Washington stood during his inauguration in 1789. The maker is unknown, but probably was American. Height, 28 3/4 inches; length, 70 inches. (Courtesy of The New-York Historical Society, New York City)*

MERCER, HENRY C. *The Dating of Old Houses, Boston: Old Time New England*, Bulletin of the Society for the Preservation of New England Antiquities, April 1924.

MILLER, JOHN. Manuscript daybook of John Miller, blacksmith in Lancaster, Pennsylvania, 1744-1764.

MOXON, JOSEPH. *Mechanick Exercises; or the Doctrine of Handy-Works.* London: Printed for D. Midwinter and Thos. Leigb, 1703.

ORCUTT, SAMUEL. *The History of the Old Town of Derby, Connecticut, 1642-1880. With Biographies and Genealogies.* Springfield, Mass., 1880.

PATTEN, MATTHEW. Manuscript diary of Matthew Patten. Bedford, New Hampshire, 1754-1788.

SONN, ALBERT. *Early American Wrought Iron.* New York: Charles Scribner's Sons, 1928.

SILCOCK, ARNOLD and AYRTON, MAXWELL, *Wrought Iron and Its Decorative Uses.* New York: Charles Scribner's Sons, 1929.

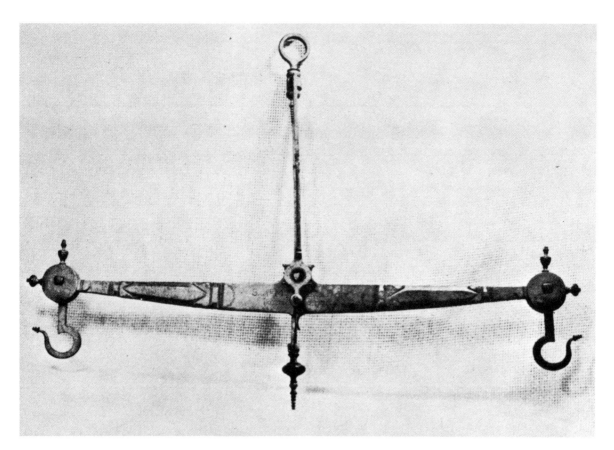

Plate 104. *Scale beam engraved:*
*"Samuel McClench fecit, Boston*
*1779." The unusual filed and*
*engraved patterns indicate it as*
*the product of a whitesmith.*
*(Courtesy of Stamford Museum*
*and Nature Center) Plate 105.*
*Advertisement of Hamilton Ha-*
*zleton in Kline's Carlisle Gazette,*
*March 2, 1798. Note that the*
*variety of objects he made were*
*all filed and finished "bright".*
*His rural location suggests that he*
*probably was quite busy making*
*metal appendages for spinning*
*wheels. (Courtesy the American*
*Antiquarian Society)*

# HAMILTON HAZLETON, WHITE-SMITH.

TAKES the liberty to inform his friends and the public in general, that he makes all kinds of Truss for the Rupture, Trepanning in-struments, Tooth drawers, and all kinds of Doctor's instruments—likewise Lock making, Spindles and handles for Spin-ning Wheels, in the town of Milford, on the Walnut Bottom road, six miles from Shippensburgh, and fourteen from Carlisle.

April 9th, 1798.

# CHAPTER FIVE

# The Whitesmith

IT SHOULD BE NOTED AT THE beginning of this discussion of the white-smith that, of all the craftsmen who work-ed in metals throughout the eighteenth and nineteenth centuries, few people und-erstand precisely what this craftsman did. The trade is not mentioned in important books such as *Bishop's History of American Manufactures,* Philadelphia, 1864; nor does Carl Bridenbaugh include it in his recent book, *The Colonial Craftsman,* New York, 1950. Most dictionaries do not list the trade and there are conflicting statements in those that do include it. The definition in the *Oxford English Dictionary,* Oxford, 1933 is as follows:

 a. A worker in white iron; a tinsmith.
 b. One who polishes or finishes metal goods, as distinguished from one who forges them; also more widely, a worker in metals.

Part of the problem of precisely identify-ing the work of the whitesmith arises from the fact that many of them worked simul-taneously at other trades. An advertisement in the *Pittsburgh Gazette,* August 4, 1789, illustrates a logical combination of other trades with whitesmithing.

WANTED
An apprentice of about 14 years of age to learn the Blacksmith, Whitesmith, and Cutlery Business. En-quire of Thomas Wylie at the corner of Market and Third Streets, Pittsburgh.

These trades, with the addition of lock mak-ing, are natural combinations with white-smithing because all of them involve work-ing with iron and steel. It would be quite unreasonable and hence one rarely finds the trades of silversmithing, tinsmithing, and pewter making combined with whitesmith-ing. These latter craftsmen do work with white metals but procedures and products have little in common with those who work in iron.

It is obvious that the trade of the copper-smith and the brazier are saved from this confusion only because the metals with which they work are not white.

The research of the trade of whitesmithing focuses attention on two conclusions. The first one is that whitesmithing was essentially a trade followed in the cities. The Martin survey of craftsmen working in Bucks County, Pennsylvania, between 1750 and 1800 reveals that not one whitesmith was

81

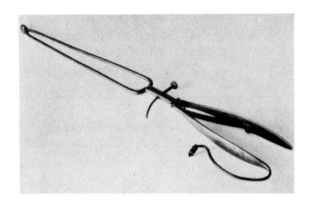

working there at that time, but the *New Trade Directory of Philadelphia for 1800* lists 22 whitesmiths working in a nearby city. An interesting exception to this conclusion is an advertisement which appeared in Kline's *Carlisle (Pa.) Gazette,* May 2, 1798:

HAMILTON HAZLETON
WHITESMITH

Takes this liberty to inform his friends and the public in general, that he makes all kinds of Trusses for the Rupture, Trepanning instruments, Tooth drawers, and all kinds of Doctor's instruments—likewise Lockmaking, Spindles and Handles for Spinning Wheels, in the town of Millford, on the Walnut Bottom Road, six miles from Shippensburg, and fourteen from Carlisle.

The second conclusion is that, in addition to several allied fringe trades such as bell hanging and smoke-jack making, there was another type of work unique to the trade. This opinion is supported by an advertisement of George McGunnigle in the *Pittsburgh Gazette,* August 1, 1789:

The subscriber respectfully informs the public that he has moved his shop to the house formerly occupied by Mr. Marmaduke Curtis, in Market Street, where he carried on the Black & Whitesmith Business. He has furnished himself with a very good horseshoer and country smith and likewise makes locks and key hinges of all sorts, pipe tomahawks, scalping knives, boxes and pins for vizes, grates, polished and

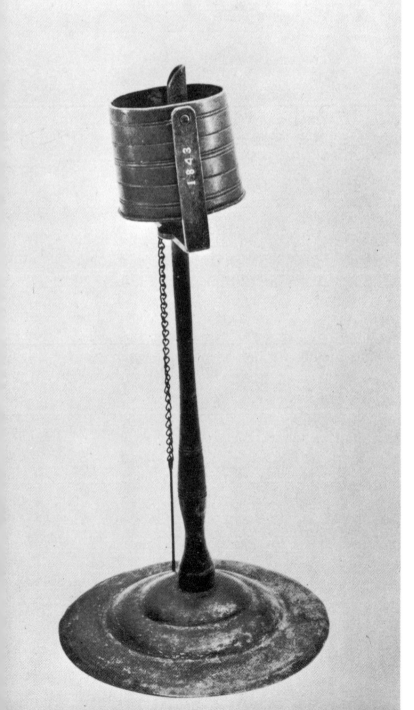

Plate 107. *Standing fluid lamp having an iron stand and a cup and chain of brass, marked "P.D." on one side of the bracket and "1843" on the other. The "P.D." stands for Peter Derr of Reading, Pennsylvania, who was a prolific lamp maker in the mid-19th century. (Courtesy of the Pennsylvania Historical and Museum Commission, Harrisburg, Pennsylvania)*

Plate 108. *Iron candle snuffers of unusual design, possibly of the 18th century. Although brass snuffers of this type are not uncommon, iron ones are unique. The maker and the origin of these snuffers are not known, but objects of this type probably were made by American whitesmiths. (Kauffman Collection)*

or his associate, did horse shoeing and other work done by a "country smith." The logical conclusion follows that McGunnigle was the whitesmith and the nature of the objects

unpolished and irons, shovels, tongs, pokers, chaffing dishes, bread toasters, ladles, skimmers, flesh forks and skewers, with all kinds of iron work for kitchens, currying combs, plates, saddle trees, makes crapeing, curbing, and pincing tongs, rupture belts, grinds swords, razors, scissors, and pen knives, cleans and polishes guns and pistols. As he is determined to do any of the above work on the most reasonable terms, he flatters himself he will engage the attention and favors of the public.

GEORGE McGUNNIGLE

September 15...makes bed screws and branding irons of all sizes and does several other pieces of business in the Whitesmith line, too tedious to mention. He also carries on the Blacksmith, in the shop late occupied by William Braden, in partnership with James Beard, who is perfectly well qualified for horse shoeing of any kind of work in that way, also makes horse, cow and sheep bells.

GEORGE McGUNNIGLE

The McGunnigle advertisements in the *Pittsburgh Gazette* call attention to the fact that two trades were followed in his shop, whitesmithing and blacksmithing. He points out in both advertisements that his employee

Plate 109. *Bread toaster signed by Mead and Havens, which appears to be the product of a blacksmith and a whitesmith. It is interesting to note that Longworth's New York Directory for 1831-32 lists two blacksmiths named Meade and a whitesmith named John Havens. An object signed by this combination of craftsmen probably is unique. (Kauffman Collection)*

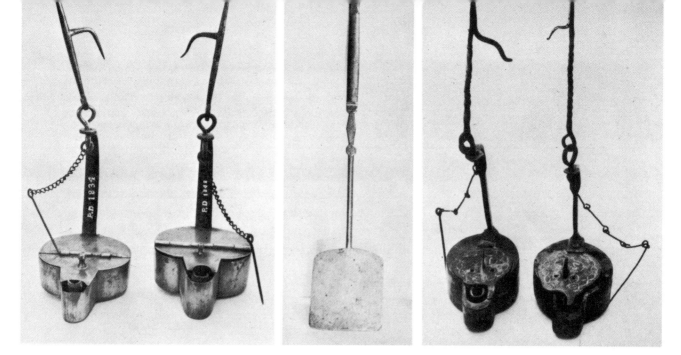

Plate 110. *Brass fat lamps made by Peter Derr in 1834 and 1848. The supporting strap and hook are of iron. It is evident that styles in fat lamps did not change very much between these dates. The lamps are in unusually good condition and are well marked. (Courtesy of the Pennsylvania Historical and Museum Commission, Harrisburg, Pennsylvania)* Plate 111. *Iron spatula probably made by a blacksmith and finished by a whitesmith. Whitesmiths also made a great many forks, dippers, and ladles. (John Evans, Jr. Collection)* Plate 112. *Iron fat lamps made of sheet iron by John Long, the one on the left in 1832 and that on the right in 1835. Note the attractive punched decoration on the lids and the initials "J.S." standing for their first owner. Lamps such as these usually were finished bright and were assembled with the use of hard solder. (Courtesy of the Pennsylvania Historical and Museum Commission, Harrisburg, Pennsylvania)*

listed in the advertisement suggests that they were his products.

Of all the trades combined with whitesmithing under one roof, blacksmithing was the most frequent and logical; for the work of the whitesmith was the filing, polishing, and assembling of objects made by the blacksmith. It appears that the blacksmith roughly formed such objects as irons, firetools, skimmers, rupture belts, etc. The finishing of these products required a more refined type of workmanship than is usually associated with blacksmithing, so they were passed on to the whitesmith. The whitesmith filed and polished the surfaces, possibly heat-treated some of them, and then carefully fitted them together with rivets or by brazing. He probably turned them on a lathe, fastened brass handles supplied by the brass founder, and possibly also did some chasing and engraving.

In conclusion, it should be mentioned that there were times when the forging and finishing of objects made of iron were probably done by one man, but it is very evident that these two distinct trades were involved in the making of many objects of iron.

BIBLIOGRAPHY

GOTTESHAM, RITA SUSSWEIN, compiler. *The Arts and Crafts in New York, 1726-1776.* New York: New York Historical Society, 1938.

CHAPTER SIX

# The Farrier

THE *OXFORD ENGLISH DICTION-ary,* Oxford 1933, defines a farrier as "One who shoes horses; a shoeing smith; hence, also one who treats the disease of horses." Although this word seems to have an English origin, it is recorded in the dictionary mentioned above that the trade was started in Germany. The common use of the word in England is supported by the fact that a *General Directory of Kingston-Upton-Hull and the City of York,* 1846, indicates that at that time, thirty-four blacksmiths and farriers were working in Hull and eleven blacksmiths and two farriers were working in York. It is also interesting to note that the term farrier was frequently used in the English colonies of New England, but rarely used in the German settlement of Lancaster, Pennsylvania.

It is obvious from the research done on the trade that the farrier was frequently a general blacksmith, a maker of shoes and a shoer of horses, and one who treated the diseases of the horse. The work of the general blacksmith has been discussed at an earlier time

in this survey, and the treating of diseases does not fall within the scope of this study; so the main subject to be considered at this time is the making of shoes and the shoeing of horses.

It appears that as early as 1750, the farrier secured his iron from a rolling and slitting mill in a form and size that did not require a great deal of work; however, the making of a correct shoe for a hoof with abnormalities was a more complicated matter. Today, horse-shoe making often involves so-called "orthopedic" work and it is likely that some of this work was done in the eighteenth and nineteenth centuries.

Making a shoe did not require a great deal of manual skill. In a record of *Indentures of Individuals Bound Out as Apprentices, Servants, Etc.* recorded in the Office of the Mayor of the City of Philadelphia from October 3, 1771 to October 5, 1773, blacksmiths served an average time of six years while craftsmen such as saddlers, cordwainers, goldsmiths, and whitesmiths served an apprenticeship period ranging from seven to twelve years in length.

85

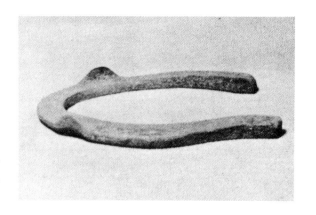

It should also be noted that the blacksmith was taught to do many types of work in addition to the making of shoes and the shoeing of horses. There are no cases included of men who became only farriers; however, if there were, their period of apprenticeship would probably not have been longer than two or three years.

There probably were as many ways to make a horse shoe as there were men making them; however, the procedure outlined here suggests one way in which a shoe could be made. A bar of iron $5/16'' \times 3/4'' \times 12''$ was cut from a bar with a hammer and a hardy. The ends of the bar were forged on the face of the anvil until they were reduced in width and increased in thickness. The bar was then roughly shaped into a U over the horn of the anvil. Few shoes made by hand were creased, but that operation followed if it were to be done. Holes were punched from the bottom side of the shoe and these were tapered so that when the head of the nail was worn away, the nail continued to hold the shoe on

the horse's foot. Punching the holes distorted the shape of the shoe so it had to be reheated and reshaped. A small clip was forged on the toe end of the shoe to help keep the shoe properly positioned on the hoof. Heel calks were next welded on the two heel portions of the shoe. After cutting the ends square, the shoe was forged smooth at all points and laid aside until all the shoes were made.

The proper preparation of the foot to receive the new shoe was a matter of much importance in the shoeing operation. The old shoe was attached by driving nails through the shoe and the hoof, and then clenched over the hoof. Careless farriers often removed only a few of the clenched ends and then with a violent wrench separated the shoe from the foot. Such a procedure caused nail holes to be unduly enlarged and sometimes part of the hoof was broken away. Sometimes portions of nails were left which caused much trouble if they were not carefully removed with a punch.

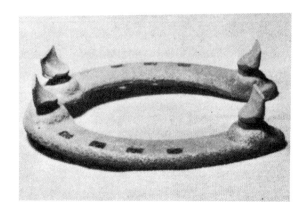

Plate 114. *Massive horseshoe equipped with four calks to prevent slipping on ice. The chisel-shaped calks were press-fitted to facilitate replacement when worn smooth.*

Plate 115. *Various shapes and sizes of horseshoes made today by a blacksmith near Philadelphia, Pennsylvania. (Courtesy of George Basinger)*

The hoof then had to be carefully pared to receive the new shoe. Few horses became lame because of poor workmanship on the shoes, but many were made uncomfortable and were injured because of indiscreet paring operations. Proper fitting was done by shaping the shoe rather than by unreasonable paring of the hoof. If the hoof were thinned where nails were placed, the danger of injury was greatly increased. It is known that some ignorant or careless farriers fitted shoes by heating them and pressing them against the foot of the horse. In this procedure, more of the hoof was removed than was usually necessary, and all critics view such an act as one of abuse and poor judgment.

It is not known when manufactured horse shoes became available to the farrier, but today most of them buy factory-made shoes and shoe horses with them. There is some use of aluminum shoes today for racing horses and we may go the "full circle" some day and return to silver shoes like the ones Nero used on his horses.

BIBLIOGRAPHY
*General Directory of Kingston-Upton, Hull and City of York.* Sheffield: F. White & Co. 1846.
*Record of Indentures of Individuals Bound Out as Ap-* *prentices, Servants, etc., in Philadelphia, Penna.* by Mayor John Gibson, 1771-72, Mayor William Fisher, 1773. Norristown, Pa.: The Pennsylvania German Society Proceedings, XVI, 1907.

Plate 116. *Iron tools for cutting and handling ice, exhibited in the "New Jersey Iron, 1764-1850" display at Trenton, New Jersey. The collection includes an axe, a cutter, a pair of tongs, a hatchet, a hook and a pickaxe. (Courtesy of the New Jersey State Museum)*

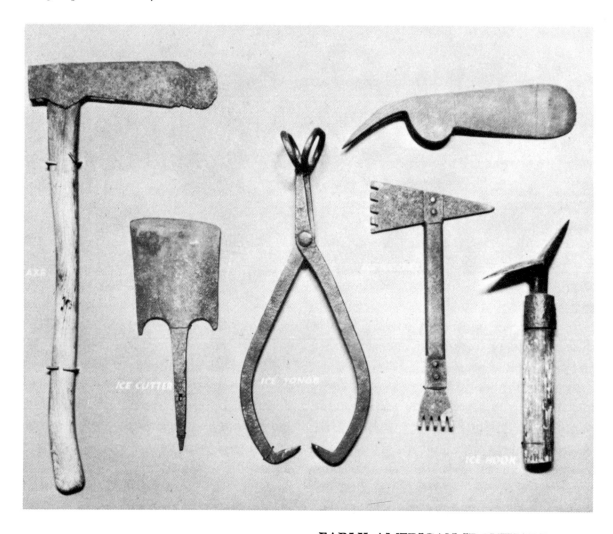

# CHAPTER SEVEN

# The Edge Toolmaker

ANOTHER IMPORTANT FACET OF blacksmithing in the seventeenth, eighteenth, and nineteenth centuries was the art of edge tool-making. This business was pursued mostly by city blacksmiths, and there are numerous entries in the business directories of cities along the eastern seaboard of men who specialized in this type of work. A typical advertisement of such a craftsman appeared in the *Pennsylvania Packet and Daily Advertiser,* July 7, 1789:

Wm. PERKINS, Blacksmith
Makes and sells at his shop in Water street, next door to the corner, above South street, in Philadelphia, the following ARTICLES; and has now by him a Quantity of the best Kind of WOOD or Falling Axes, Broad Axes, Adzes, Carpenters' mauls, Hatchets of different kinds, Ditching or Banking Shovels, Weeding or Corn Hoes, Grubbing Hoes, Tucking Hoes, Chissels, Plane Irons, 10d and 12d Nails, Hooks and Hinges, and many other Articles too tedious to mention.

The equipment needed for this type of work closely resembled that of an ordinary blacksmith. The forge was equipped with bellows, operated by hand, and there was the customary number hammers, sledges, tongs, and an anvil. The iron was heated to a bright red heat if the object of the work were to reduce the form of the iron. A red heat was used to weld two pieces together and a slightly lower temperature was used if the internal structure of the iron were to be made more compact or the surface smoothed. The large piece of iron needed to make tools like broad axes and mattocks required more than one man to forge the metal when it was hot. The most experienced man managed the metal in the forge and on the anvil, while he and his helpers struck it with sledges before it cooled below the working temperature. The assistants (called strikers) were usually apprentices or unskilled blacksmiths. There was a slightly different procedure used in the forging of shovels and hoes. The hammering was done by a huge hammer motivated by water power, called a trip-hammer.

The shape of edge tools has changed very little from early times; however, it should be noted that some of the materials of which

89

they are made have changed as well as the methods used to make them. Most of the tools of the seventeenth, eighteenth, and nineteenth centuries were made of iron and "blister steel." This combination was used because they could be forged on a small

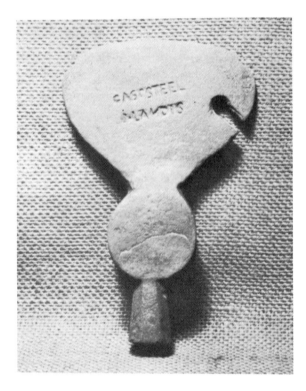

forge; such production was based on an economy in which iron was a common commodity and steel was a scarce one, and because the final product was quite satisfactory from an aesthetic and functional point of view.

To make a tool like an axe, two thin pieces of iron were welded together, allowing an undersize hole for the handle in one end of the tool and shaping a V or a bevel on the other end, to which a piece of steel would later be welded. This work could be done on a small forge, for there the slabs of iron could be heated until the outer surfaces were pasty for welding and the inner parts stayed rigid to maintain the rough shape of the tool. After the two pieces were welded together, a mandrel was used to enlarge and properly shape the hole for the handle. A piece of blister steel was properly shaped and welded to the other end and forged to a reasonably sharp edge. The surfaces of the axe were

Plate 118. *Old hatchets, in comparison with old axes, are very scarce. This one obviously was made of cast steel by a man named Landis. Although "cast steel" was frequently stamped on tools made of it, the stamping seldom was as evident. (Kauffman Collection)*

Plate 119. *Broad axe made by J. B. Stohler of Lancaster County, Pennsylvania. The different texture of the cutting edge indicates that the body was made of iron and the cutting edge of steel. (Kauffman Collection)*

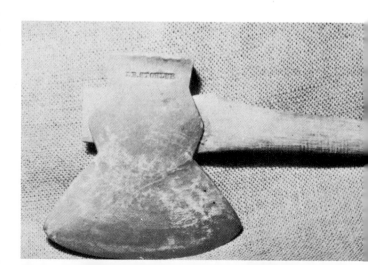

Plate 120. *Cooper's tools made by the L. and I. J. White Company of Buffalo, New York. (Courtesy of the Essex Institute, Salem, Massachusetts) The following account of this interesting firm is extracted from the book* Buffalo of To-day, The Queen City of the Lakes *published by the Interstate Publishing Company, Buffalo and Chicago, in 1892: "One of the old established, always successful and flourishing industries of Buffalo is the extensive edge tool factory... established at Monroe, Michigan, in 1837 by Mr. Leonard White, but Buffalo had already begun to attract manufacturers, and seven years later his operations were transferred to this point and he was joined by his brother, the late Mr. I. J. White. The result has more than fulfilled expectations. For twenty-four years the firm occupied large premises on Exchange Street, corner of Perry. The new manufactory is fitted up with great care as to economy of time and labor and is certainly one of the largest and best equipped in the country. The finest machinery obtainable is in use, and the manufacture of fine edge tools has been brought to a point where the superior excellence of their goods places them in a most enviable position. Mr. Leonard White, of this widely-known firm, is the oldest practical edge-tool man in America. The implements manufactured embrace cooper's, butcher's, carpenter's and ship-carpenter's tools of every imaginable description, including a full line of chisels and a great variety of machine knives embracing planing, molding, stave, hoop, veneer, paper-cutting, leather-splitting, and shear blades for cutting metal, the quality of which has created a world-wide demand for them. Their exhibit won the Paris Exposition medal of 1889. The present officers of the company are Leonard White, president; Mrs. I. J. White, vice-president; J. W. Best, treasurer and general manager, and J. W. White, superintendent."*

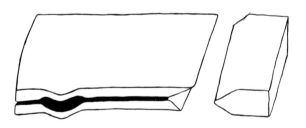

Plate 121. *Sketch showing the method of making an axe from three pieces of metal, two of iron and one of steel. After the parts were joined the hole for the handle was enlarged and the cutting edge was forged and ground.*

hammered smooth. The steel edge of the bit was only an inch to two inches wide and, after being sharpened many times, the steel was ground away. The axe was then taken to a toolmaker or a blacksmith, who "laid" another piece of steel on the axe.

One of the first famous mechanics in America, named Joseph Jenks, built a forge on the property of the Saugus Furnace. There he made a variety of edge tools. In May, 1655, he was given a patent for the improvement and manufacture of scythes. His scythe had a turned-back edge to strengthen it, and the shape has undergone little change from

then until today. In 1652, he made dies for coinage and his pine-tree imprint on old coins is familiar to all school children who study the history of early America.

Another notable person, Hugh Orr, moved to Bridgewater, Massachusetts, in 1738. He later trained as a locksmith and a gunsmith, but his fame in Bridgewater rested on the products of his trip hammer. For several years, he was the only maker of edge tools in the area, and shipwrights and carpenters constantly visited him to buy his products. His son, Robert Orr, continued the making of scythes and shovels with a trip hammer. In 1804, Robert was master armorer at the National Arsenal at Springfield, Massachusetts.

The next change in the production of edge tools was the substitution of cast steel for blister steel. Blister steel was made by a pro-cess called "cementation." It was made in a furnace shaped like a large rectangular box, or trough, with a grate in the bottom having a number of vertical flues. A layer of charcoal dust was sprinkled on the grate. Layers of bar iron were laid on the dust, with dust in between them so that one bar could not touch another. There were alternate layers of charcoal and iron until the box was filled. The top of the box was covered with clay to prevent the introduction of foreign materials and the fire was started under the grate. The process required a week for bringing the temperature to the desired heat and for cooling. In this process, the pure iron absorbed enough carbon from the charcoal to convert it to steel. The surface of the bars was covered with puffs or blisters and the metal was then called blister steel. Since the carbon was not evenly absorbed, the steel required considerable forging before it could be used.

In the 1760's, an Englishman devised a way to eliminate the irregular qualities of blister steel. He broke the brittle steel into small pieces and packed them in a crucible which was made reasonably airtight. The crucibles were placed in a furnace under a hot blast for several days, until the mass of metal was completely molten and the chemical composition made uniform. The crucibles were then removed from the furnace and the metal cast in small ingots which were later reheated and forged. This metal was called "cast steel" and it replaced blister steel as a metal for use in the edge of tools used for

Plate 123. *Five adzes with various polls for different uses. The one on the left has been identified as a carpenter's adze and the one on the right as a ship-carpenter's. Experts fail to agree regarding the specific functions of the remaining three. (Kauffman Collection)*

cutting. Few, if any, tools were made with cast steel in the eighteenth century in America.

The production of edge tools in the latter part of the nineteenth century is described in Appleton's *Cyclopedia of Applied Mechanics,* New York, 1880. It explained that an axe was made of a portion of high-quality rolled iron, cut to shape with heavy shears. The blanks were partially formed by rollers and then welded together under the trip hammer, leaving an opening in the end of the axe to receive the steel edge. The axe and the steel insert were then reheated and welded together under a powerful trip hammer. The form was finally shaped and trued by hand-hammering. The axes were then heated to a cherry-red and dropped into a brine solution. After a superficial cleaning, they were tempered by reheating them indirectly to a temperature of a "pigeon-blue" color. Finally, a short handle extending on each side of the axe was inserted so that the final grinding could be done on huge emery wheels. These wheels were about four feet in diameter when they were new. The worker who did the grinding sat on a high stool and cleverly held the axe in a variety of positions for the final grinding. Sprays of sparks 6 to 8 feet long left the wheel and made a very dramatic sight in the semi-darkened room. Handles were then installed and a portion of the axe was painted.

The shape of an axe was influenced by the type of wood on which it was to be used; however, woodcutters throughout America and the rest of the world have personal preferences for certain shapes.

The extensive description of the making of an axe should not lead the reader to think that no other edge tools were made by this craftsman in iron. The following advertisement from a *Baltimore Business Directory* of 1850 indicates the range of tools made at that time:

Edge tools were made by hand or in small

Plate 124. *Broad cast steel axe made by Sener in Lancaster, Pennsylvania bearing his usual eagle imprint. (Vincent Nolt Collection)*

# CHARLES KIDD,
## CAST STEEL
## EDGE TOOL FACTORY,
### *No. 352 W. Pratt street, (Sign of the Axe,)*
#### (BETWEEN GREEN AND PENN,)
## BALTIMORE,

Where may be found a good assortment of Ship Carpenters' Axes, Adzes, Chisels, &c. House Carpenters' Hand Axes, Hatchets, Chisels, &c. Mill Wrights' Broad Axes, Adzes, Chisels, Gouges, &c. Coopers' Axes, Adzes, Drawing, Rounding and Hollowing Knives, &c. Block Makers' Round Axes, Gouges and Chisels. Masons' Hammers, Picks, Mattoxes, Grubing Hoes, Stone Sledges and Quarry Tools.

All kinds of Mill Work made and repaired in the best manner.

Orders for Axes, Tools, or Iron Work of any kind thankfully received and promptly attended to.

All persons in want of tools, will do well to call and judge for themselves.

*Plate 125. Advertisement of Charles Kidd in a Baltimore Business Directory for 1850, showing the variety of edge tools made at that time.*

factories using hand methods until the middle of the twentieth century. One case is known in Pennsylvania where water power was detached about 1930 from the hammers and electric motors were installed. Tools were still ground by hand on a huge wheel, as had been done for a century or two. It is interesting to note that a tool for hand use defied machine production for such a long time.

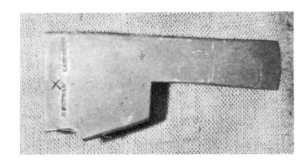

*Plate 126. Axes were made in various shapes according to the use to be made of them. This one, known as a "post-hole" axe, was made in Lancaster, Pennsylvania by a craftsman named S. Hofman. (Kauffman Collection)*

### BIBLIOGRAPHY
BENJAMIN, PARK, Ed. *Appleton's Cyclopedia of Applied Mechanics*. 2 vols. New York: D. Appleton and Company, 1880.
BISHOP, J. LEANDER. *A History of American Manufactures from 1608 to 1860*. Philadelphia: Edward Young & Company, 1861.
*The Great Industries of the United States*. New York: J. Brainard & Co., 1874.
MERCER, HENRY C. *Ancient Carpenters' Tools*. Doylestown, Pa., Bucks County Historical Society, 1951.

*Plate 127. Copy of an old print showing a mid-19th century axe factory in Cincinnati, Ohio.*

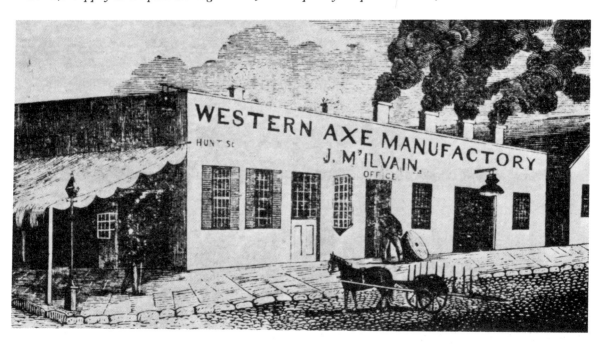

# CHAPTER EIGHT

# The Cutler

MUCH OVERLAPPING OF TRADES has been noted among all the craftsmen who worked in metals throughout the eighteenth and nineteenth centuries. The trade of the cutler was no exception to this general rule. Thomas Wylie advertised in the *Pittsburgh Gazette,* August 4, 1789, for a fourteen year old boy to learn the blacksmith, whitesmith, and cutlery business. On October 24, 1789, another advertisement in the same paper indicates that Wylie was then working as a blacksmith, whitesmith, and edge tool-maker. John Aris combined his cutlery business with whitesmithing in New York in 1742, and John Wallace was working there about the same time as a cutler who made "Kitchin furniture that belongs to the Smiths Trade." A unique trade combined with the cutlery business was that of John Sculthorpe who advertised in the *New York Gazette,* January 28, 1760, that he had been a cutler and a peruke-maker, but was giving up one of the trades. His advertisement follows:

Whereas John Sculthorpe, Peruke-maker, near the Fly Market, has for several years past, carried on the above business and Cutlery grinding, and intends now to decline one of them, as he cannot attend them with such Dispatch as he would chuse. He therefore informs any Persons of either of the said Business, that they may enter into a good accustomed shop, by applying to him, who will agree for the same on Reasonable terms.

N.B. As due attendance cannot be given to both, he hopes to serve his customers, in the continued one of Peruke-making, in a more regular and expeditious manner. To be entered into on May next.

A summary of trades combined with the cutler includes the following: blacksmith, gunsmith, brass founder, surgeon's instrument maker, sword maker, sickle and scythe maker, silversmith, forger, scale maker, and peruke-maker.

It is difficult to completely isolate the products of the cutler in this array of occupations commonly associated with the trade. The name of the trade suggests that he was a maker of small edge tools and his products include: table knives, butcher-knives, swords, sickles, scythes, lancets, buttons and

Plate 128. *Cleaver for cutting meat, made of cast steel in Economy, Pennsylvania. Cast steel was used in making many cutting-edge tools during the mid-19th century. (Courtesy of Lawrence Thurman)*

buckles, cork-screws, seals, forks, taylors shears, thimbles, cock gaffs, edge tools, pinking-irons, hatters knives, trusses, double-jointed players, smoke jacks, shoemakers knives, fullers sheers, brass buckles, brass boxes for mill brushes, "kitchin" furniture, irons for lame legs, leg irons for children with crooked feet, instruments for setting teeth, steel back stays and collars for young ladies, iron work for saw and grist mills, and steel collars for children.

The advertisement of James Youle in *London's New-York Packet,* February 3, 1785, suggests the common type of work done by a cutler, except for one which he calls "steel collars for children." This product might logically be an interesting topic to research, but time does not permit including such work in this survey.

JAMES YOULE, cutler, informs his friends and the public in general, that he has removed from the Fly Market to No. 64 Water-street, corner of Beekman Slip; where he carries on his business as usual; makes all sorts of surgeons instruments, trusses for ruptures, steel collars for children, irons for lame legs, silversmith's tools, phlegms, razors, knives, skeats, (sic), and all sorts of gunwork; likewise grinds all sorts of cutlery, cuts gentlemen's and ladies names for printing linens and books, gives red or black ink, which will not wash out, and may be used by any person without inconveniency; likewise cuts brands for branding casks; etc. He has just imported for sale, a large assortment of hardware and cutlery, and a few pairs of the best blacksmiths and silversmiths bellows, which he will sell on the most moderate terms.

An item in the *New-York Packet,* February 27, 1786, reports that Mr. Youle met an untimely death in this shop when a large grinding wheel which he was using broke

Plate 129. *Iron halberd, possibly American. Halberds more often served as a symbol of office than as a functional weapon. (Kauffman Collection)*

**EARLY AMERICAN IRONWARE ✦ 96**

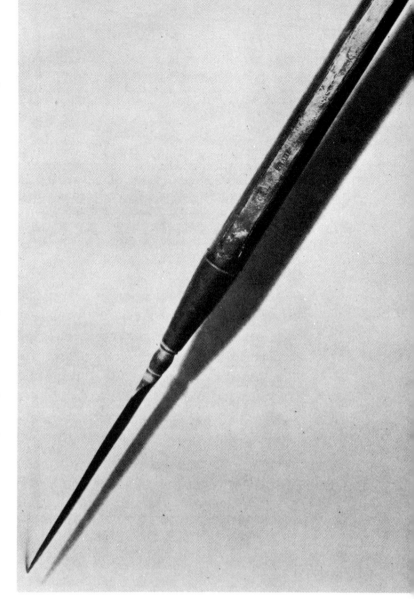

into four parts and one part hit him on the breast. The report concluded by saying that, "He was an ingenious mechanic, a peaceable, honest, and useful citizen and has left a widow with nine children to deplore his loss."

A survey of the advertisements of cutlers suggests that these men did two types of work. The advertisement of Mr. Youle indicates that he was a tradesman who might be logically called a manufacturing-cutler. The major part of his work was the making of objects, but he also did some custom sharpening for his customers. The other type of cutler might be called a merchant-cutler. This man's trade was concerned with the selling of cutlery and the sharpening of tools. The advertisement of Richard Sause in the *New York Gazette*, April 6–13, 1767, indicates that he was a merchant-cutler. He does not mention that he made cutlery.

RICHARD SUASE, cutler, has removed from the corner of the Slote, in Smith-street, next door to Messers Thompson's and Selby's Saddlers, near the coffee house, where he continues to carry on the cutlery business, in its various branches. Viz-New works of various sorts, surgeon's instruments of all

Plate 131. *Lancet with iron blade in a brass case. Lancets ranged in length from two to six inches. Many were signed by their makers, of whom there were many in in Philadelphia and New York.*

97 ✦ THE CUTLER

Plate 132. *Pocket knife, probably early 19th century, with wooden curly maple handle. While this one has but one blade, others made at that time had a great many. (Park Emery Collection)*

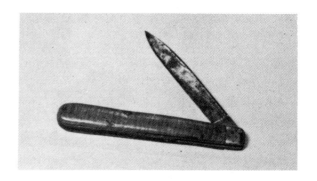

sorts, ground, glazed, polished, and set, swords, pistols, guns, &c. cleaned and polished, silversmith's, brazier's, and tinmen's tools of all sorts ground and polished; taylors, glovers, and all other shears; chopping knives, sadllers, shoemakers, and butcher knives; fleams razors, scissors, pen knives, (and any other things to tedious to mention) ground and finished in a neat manner.

The early use of knives and other tools for cutting suggests that the cutler was one of the earliest craftsmen working in metals. It is evident from archaelogical research that the shape of cutting tools varied from time to time, and place to place; however, it is likely that some common procedures were used by all craftsmen. It is known that similar techniques were used in the making of tool such as knives, swords, scythes, sickles, and razors.

No ancient records are known which describe precisely how the early cutting tools were made, but the mode of producing objects by hand changed very little before machine production was invented. *Knight's Pictorial Gallery of the Arts,* published in London about the middle of the nineteenth century gives insight into the techniques used by craftsmen in the hand production of cutting tools.

The universal shape and function of the knife suggests that a description of its production might provide a basic formula for the making of other similar tools. A blank of steel was first secured the approximate size and shape of the intended blade. The metal was heated to a forging temperature and the blade forged to the shape desired. The blade was then welded to an iron rod (to conserve steel) and the rod was forged into the common form of a knife tang. Extra metal was also provided on the end of the iron rod to form the shoulder which divided the blade from the handle. The final forging included the shaping of the shoulder and the smoothing of the knife blade. The blade was hardened by again heating it to a red heat and dropping it into a cask of cold water; after which it was partially reheated for the tempering operation.

Plate 133. *Knives and forks with handles of horn, made by J. Ashmore, Philadelphia, Pennsylvania, listed as a cutler residing at 50 North Second Street in 1840. (Courtesy of the Deerfield Historical Museum)*

**EARLY AMERICAN IRONWARE ✦ 98**

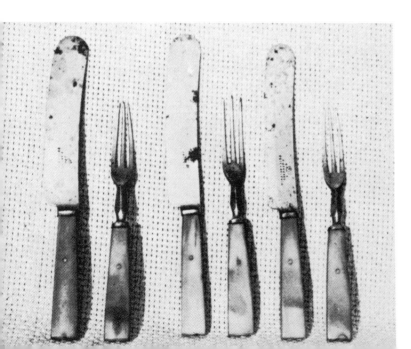

Plate 134. *Drawing of the Green River Works near Greenfield, Massachusetts. Much of the cutlery made in America in the 19th century was made at this place. (Courtesy of the Deerfield Historical Museum)*

At this point, the blade was still oversize in thickness and contour. The first grinding was done on a large stone, three to four feet in diameter, where it was thinned and the contour refined to its final shape. The second stone on which the blade was ground was very fine and because it produced a white texture on the blade, it was called a whitening-stone. Final polishing was done on a wheel made of wood and covered with a piece of leather. The leather was coated with glue in which was imbedded fine grains of abrasive powder. Worn wheels of the last type imparted the final and highest polish to the blade. The metal part of the knife was fitted with a handle of ivory, wood, bone, silver, mother of pearl, or horn.

There were only a few different procedures in the making of a razor blade from the making of a knife blade. The blade was

Plates 135-6. *American sword made by N. Starr, who had several government contracts for edged weapons in the early decades of the 19th century. A great many of his products were signed, some of which were also dated. (Fredrick Monkhouse Collection)*

matter of hardness and tempering in all tools was determined by the color of the steel in the tempering operation. The temperatures for different types of work follows:

| Fahr. | | |
|---|---|---|
| 600 | Blackish blue | } Springs |
| 560 | Blue | |
| 550 | Bright blue | } { Pocket knives |
| 530 | Purple | Table knives |
| 510 | Brown with purple spots | } { Scissors |
| 490 | Brown | } Pen knives |
| 470 | Yellow | |
| 450 | Pale straw | } { Razors |
| 430 | Slight yellow | } { Lancets |

forged before it was severed from the bar of metal. All operations were performed in a more critical manner. Much care was required in the hardening and tempering operations for if the razor were too hard, the edge became too brittle; and if it were too soft, it could not be sharpened to a keen edge. The

The making of scissors involved problems similar to those in the making of a knife. Some handles were made by elongating the bar of metal and shaping it into the hand grip. Others were made by punching a hole in the sheet stock from which the blade was to be made and then enlarging the hole to a "hand-grip" shape and size. The anvil of the scissors maker was fitted with various appendages designed to shape the open handles of the scissors. Large scissors had blades made of steel and handles of iron to conserve the restricted supply of steel and reduce the cost. The grinding and polishing was done on wheels similar to those used for knives and the final operation was riveting, or bolting, the two parts together.

One would naturally suspect that within the trade of the cutler, certain specialists would work in making only one or two types of tools. There is evidence that a separate trade of sickle and scythe making existed in many parts of America. William Dawson, a cutler in Philadelphia, advertised his specialty by having a sickle and the blade of a scythe illustrated in his newspaper advertisement in the *Pennsylvania Evening Post*, April 13, 1767. He also emphasizes scythes and sickles in the contents of his advertisement:

WILLIAM DAWSON
CUTLER, at the sign of the Scythe and the Sickle, in Third-street, between Market and Arch Streets, Philadelphia, makes in the best Manner, and sells on reasonable terms.
  Scythes, Sickles, Iron Works for Grist and Saw Mills, Chocolate Mills, Smiths Bellows, Steelyards, etc.

The work in scythes and sickles was of much importance in rural Pennsylvania which was settled by people who had earlier experiences in agricultural procedures in central Europe. The shape of their scythe was probably not unique, but they did have a unique set of tools which were used for sharpening their scythes. It consisted of a number of small anvils and a hammer. These anvils had a point on one end so that they could be driven into a tree stump or other massive piece of wood. The other end was suited to a variety of sharpening procedures, either for thinning the blade or for serrating it by placing the blade on the anvil and striking it on the top with a hammer. The set also included a sheath of wood or horn in which a whetstone was carried. The sheath was filled with water and hooked on the operator's belt or other part of his apparel. Similar equipment was probably used in other parts of rural America; however, sets of these tools seem to have been used longer in Pennsylvania and more have survived there than in other places.

The making of swords was also a highly specialized type of work done by some cutlers. The problems of knife making were met again by the swordmaker with some additional ones peculiar to the trade. A high grade of metal was reqoired for the extensive operations on the forge and for the subsequent hardening and tempering. Finishing was done in a meticulous manner and the decorating of sword blades called for skill and artistic talent. Probably some sword forgers made hilts, but certainly the silver ones were made by silversmiths. There is evidence that many men made cutlery, but sword makers were rare in America. Sword makers were the most highly skilled men in the cutlery trade.

BIBLIOGRAPHY
HIMSWORTH, J. B. *The Story of Cutlery*, London: Ernest Benn, 1953.
*The Pictorial Gallery of Arts*. London and New York: Printed and Published by The London Printing and Publishing Co., 1855.

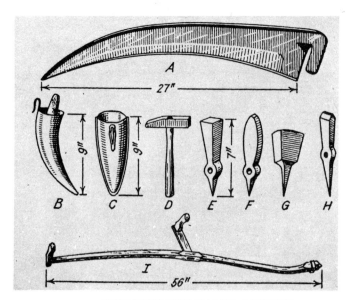

THE PENNSYLVANIA SCYTHE

No collector or student of agricultural tools can have failed to be deeply interested in the mowing outfit of the early Pennsylvania-German farmer. It included a scythe blade *(dengel sense)* hard-forged from extremely malleable iron, unusually broad and thin, with the back edge turned over to form a stiffening "rib" (Fig. A). This was "hung" on a snath, of which one handhold was mortised and pegged at about its middle to the extreme end of the snath, so that the effect was that of a cross-handle, the other handhold being mortised and pegged into the end of a piece some six inches long, projecting from the snath proper, and in turn mortised to it (Fig. I). Occasionally, the natural growth of the wood was utilized to form one or both of these hand-holds. The mower also had a small hand-forged "anvil", *(dengel shtock)* usually about seven inches long and weighing about a pound (although they are known up to ten inches and four pounds), of which one end was brought to a sharp point, and the other had a flat face about an inch and a quarter square (Fig. E), or was shaped like a wedge, with a face only about three-sixteenths of an inch wide (Fig. F), and with a hole in the middle, presumably to hang it up by, when not in use. He also had a small hand-forged hammer *(dengel hammer),* with a flat face at one end of the head, and a wedge-shaped peen at the other (Fig D). When the scythe required a thorough sharpening, he drove the point of the anvil into a log or stump, and drew the blade across its face, beating out the cutting edge with his hammer. For occasional whetting, he carried a piece of fine-grained sandstone in a sheath *(wetz hahn)* which was hooked to his belt. This sheath was occasionally a hollowed-out piece of wood, but much more frequently a cow's horn, with a hand-

Plate 137. *A Pennsylvania scythe and its accessories. (Courtesy of the Early American Industries Association)*

wrought hook rivetted to it (Fig. B). Many of these bear crude decorations, or the initials of the owner, and occasionally a date, which is usually of the early 19th century. According to Dr. Henry C. Mercer *(Tools of the Nation Maker, No. 25, 31)* the sheath was filled with vinegar to keep the whetstone free from grease.

Dr. Mercer also states that the general use of these remarkable tools was discontinued in Pennsylvania about 1840, but we have recently discovered that, in modern form, the scythes, as well as sickles of similar type, are still imported from Germany and are apparently very popular in widely scattered sections of this country. Mr. S. E. Gage, while driving through New Milford, Conn., recently, noticed a man coming out of the post-office carrying one of these curiously made snaths, bright with new varnish, and ascertained from him that he had purchased it from Marugg Company, of Tracy City, Tenn. We learn from the illustrated catalogue of this concern that the blade which they sell is almost identical with the early type, although made from "German Malleable steel." The snath is of "Tennessee hickory," and differs from the old style in no essential particular, except that the handholds are secured with wire brads, instead of pegs. They also offer a steel hammer head, of which both ends are wedge-shaped, as well as one which has one flat face, but the purchaser is expected to provide his own handle,—"the end of a broomstick will answer." The steel anvils are of slightly different shape from any early ones that we have seen (Fig. G and H), but the principle is obviously the same. It is recommended that the wedge-shaped anvil be used with the flat face of the hammer, in which case "the blade is turned bottom side up and hammered from the bottom," and that the flat anvil be used with the peen of the hammer, in which case "the blade is laid flat side down on the anvil and the edge is hammered from the upper side." It is claimed that this beating of the blade "produces a wide, keen, somewhat hollow, jagged, cutting edge, at the same time hardening it * * * To prevent heating of the metal, it is well to dip the hammer in water occasionally." The whetstones are imported, and the sheaths are of galvanized iron (Fig. C). It is said that the stone "should be kept immersed in water, while in use, to keep the pores open and sharp." There is no mention of vinegar.

Reprinted from *The Chronicle,* Vol. 1, No. 8, Nov. 1934,

W. B. SPRAGUE, *Editor*

# CHAPTER NINE

# The Locksmith

IT IS EVIDENT THAT THERE WAS considerable overlapping in the metal trades of the seventeenth, eighteenth, and early nineteenth centuries. This condition was particularly true of those engaged in the "smithing" trades, for most of them used the same metal to fabricate their objects and a certain core of skills existed which most men had to have.

It is interesting to note, however, that locksmiths frequently did little other work, most of them seem to have been primarily engaged in the making of locks. There was some overlapping with gunwork, whitesmithing, bell hanging, cutlery making, and other trades but in a great many cases their lone trade was locksmithing.

This situation might be explained by the fact that, since many houses were being built in America throughout the periods of colonizations and expansion, there was obviously a heavy demand for locks in most areas. It might also be pointed out that the mechanical ingenuity and exactness required by the trade created an area of specialization which isolated the locksmith from other craftsmen in metals. This logic is supported by the entry on locks in the late eighteenth century *Encyclopedia Perthensis,* Perth (Scotland), which states:

The lock is reckoned the master-piece in smithery; a great deal of art and ingenuity being required in contriving and varying the wards, springs, bolts, etc., and adjusting them to the places they are to be used, and the various occasions of using them.

The success of the locksmith probably depended on two aspects of the lock—its appearance and the complexity of its mechanism. Because most of the locks were inclosed in a case which was mounted on the exterior of the door, it was incumbent on the locksmith to make his product attractive. Most of their cases had pleasing rectangular shapes which were sometimes, though rarely, ornamented by designs engraved on the exterior side of the outer plate. Most of the cases were made of sheet iron, while the cases for richly furnished houses were made of brass.

The knobs were generally made of brass and were either round or egg-shaped. There were usually two escutcheons on the outside of the door, one for the knob and the other for the keyhole. The earliest knobs were made of three pieces of brass. The round or egg-shaped portion was made of two halves soldered together; a back bar with a square hole in it was attached to one side so that the knob could shift the latch-bolt. Later, brass knobs seem to have been stamped from one

piece of metal, to which the back bar was attached in the usual manner.

It has been pointed out that the work of the locksmith required ingenuity and accuracy. The cases were usually fitted with a precision that suggests machine production. The front plate and the rim, or edge, of the lock were joined with small rivets, which were so perfectly fitted and turned with a hammer that their location is often difficult to detect. The various bolts were probably rough-forged and then filed to their final form. The bolts on fine locks were sometimes draw filed and polished before they were finally fitted within the case.

The ingenuity of the locksmith was challenged in the arranging of the impediments, or wards, within the lock case. These circular fins, attached to one or two plates of the lock, were placed concentrically with the keyhole and created the need for the various slots, called steps, in the bit of the key. Their value from a practical point of view was greatly overrated, for a clever "lock-picker" could take a key with a blank bit, cover the bit with wax, and quickly get the impression of the wards on the key. With the imprint of the wards on the bit, he could quickly file or saw them and open the lock. It was also possible to fabricate a key with a narrow bit with a wide end which would miss all of the wards, but still throw the lock-

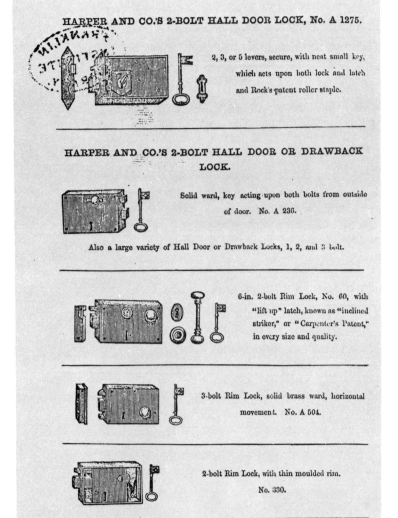

HARPER AND CO.'S 2-BOLT HALL DOOR LOCK, No. A 1275.

2, 3, or 5 levers, secure, with neat small key, which acts upon both lock and latch and Rock's patent roller staple.

HARPER AND CO.'S 2-BOLT HALL DOOR OR DRAWBACK LOCK.

Solid ward, key acting upon both bolts from outside of door. No. A 236.

Also a large variety of Hall Door or Drawback Locks, 1, 2, and 3 bolt.

6-in. 2-bolt Rim Lock, No. 60, with "lift up" latch, known as "inclined striker," or "Carpenter's Patent," in every size and quality.

3-bolt Rim Lock, solid brass ward, horizontal movement. No. A 504.

2-bolt Rim Lock, with thin moulded rim. No. 330.

2-bolt Rim Lock, rounded cast case, known as "Bailie's Patent."

Plate 138. *Page from the catalog of Harper and Company, British lock manufacturers of the mid-19th century, showing locks with two and three bolts. The third illustration from the top is of the famous "Carpenter" lock widely used in America. This had a lift latch rather than a sliding bolt as on most rim locks. (Courtesy of the Franklin Institute, Philadelphia, Pennsylvania)*

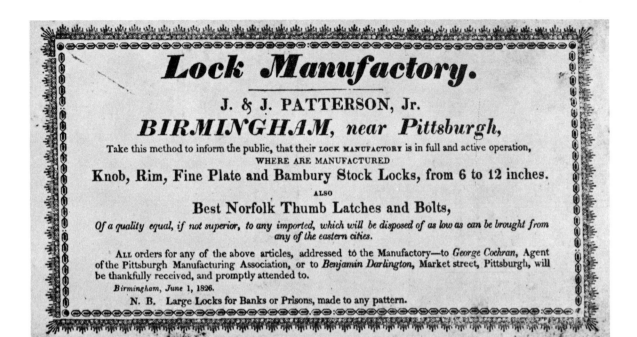

Plate 139. *Facsimile of advertisement that appeared in a business directory called* Pittsburgh *in 1826. None of the products of this manufactory have come to light although it is very likely some could be found in the Pittsburgh area. (Courtesy of the Carnegie Library of Pittsburgh, Pennsylvania)*

bolt in the usual manner. These keys were usually long and thin and were called "skeleton" keys.

It is evident that the art of key making was equally important as the making of locks. The usual door key consisted of three parts, the bit, bow, and stem. Keys were roughly forged to the approximate shape and then the lathe worker and the filer took over the work. By piercing the bow and bending it at a right angle, the stem of the key could be placed on a lathe and given a round form. Any round ornamentation on the stem was also put on at this time. The apertures in the bow and bit were formed by punching, sawing, or filing, or a combination of all three processes. A key had to be made of good metal to withstand the con-

stant pressure on the bolt, which was difficult to move at times. The best keys were made of mild steel which was soft while it was being made, but was later case-hardened. This procedure allowed the outer surface of the key to be hard and withstand much wear while the inner portion of the key was soft enough to twist before it would break. These keys were called "steel" keys.

The art of key making in America seems to have deteriorated from its earlier status in Europe. Keys for famous European buildings such as cathedrals, forts, and castles, often required weeks of work to produce the highly ornamented bows and bits. Some of these buildings have key-boards, where the various keys are displayed as works of art. Their polish and patina is evidence of some

Plate 140. *German-type door lock on the inner side of the front door of Binnagle's Church near Palmyra, Pennsylvania. This distinctive style of lock is frequently found in the Lebanon, Pennsylvania area where the Rohrer family of locksmiths worked. Obviously a "special" lock, it is completely identified by its maker. (Courtesy of Binnagle's Church)*

Plate 141. *This elaborate escutcheon is on the exterior of the front door of Binnagle's Church near Palmyra, Pennsylvania. The hole in the end of the bow of the key was to permit its insertion in a lathe. The design engraved on the handle is also typical of the fine work done by the Rohrers. (Courtesy of Binnagle's Church)*

**EARLY AMERICAN IRONWARE ✦ 106**

Plate 142. *Unique door lock with outer brass plate inscribed, "Made by D. Rohrer, 1822." The engraved motifs suggest Pennsylvania production, and the Rohrer locksmiths are known to have worked at Lebanon, Pennsylvania. (Feeman Collection)*

Plate 143. *Pennsylvania-German type door lock used in Old Salem, North Carolina. J. Misksh is believed to have been a locksmith at Bethlehem, Pennsylvania. The Salem settlement was started by Moravians from Bethlehem, and it is known that they bought objects such as locks in Bethlehem. (Courtesy of Old Salem, Inc.)*

of the finest work ever done in metals. It is difficult to determine if a key was made in America or Europe, however, no evidence has been found to support the hypothesis that many fine keys were made in America.

The most common type of door lock used in America is called a rim lock. The case and keeper were made of brass or sheet iron, and were attached to the surface of doors by nails or wood screws with round or oval heads. The locks made of iron were finished in black japan (in the nineteenth century) and the brass cases were polished "bright." In the nineteenth century many of the cases were also made of cast iron and the various bolts were made of hard brass. Broad and Green

of New York City are known to have made locks with cases of cast iron and brass bolts, about the middle of the nineteenth century.

Most of the rim locks used on outside doors were of the three-bolt type. There was a spring latch-bolt which moved horizontally with the knob. (A well known variation of this type was the English "Carpenter" lock in which the latch-bolt moved vertically instead of horizontally). The main bolt was moved with a key. When the bolt was thrown forward the door was locked, when

Plate 144. *German-type door lock with brass handles, signed by W. Clewell, a gun- and locksmith who worked in Bushkill Township, Northampton County, Pennsylvania, in 1820. Locks with brass fittings are seldom found in rural Pennsylvania. (Frank Ewing Collection)*

Plate 145. *Door lock made by D. Rohrer at Lebanon, Pennsylvania. This type is less common than the "box" type, and this particular lock is the only signed one known to exist. The spring that holds the latch bar in place is lacking. The door was locked by turning the handle on the outside of the door off the lock. Plate 146. Chest lock, possibly made by one of the Rohrer locksmiths at Lebanon, Pennsylvania. The keyhole plate is similar in shape to one used on a lock signed by Rohrer. (Kauffman Collection)*

it was thrown backward, the door was un-locked. A number of lock makers placed their trade mark on the exposed end of the lockbolt. A spring was sometimes added to the main bolt assembly to further complicate the opening of the lock by a person who did not have the correct key. A night bolt was frequently located on the bottom edge of rim locks. This bolt could be operated only by hand on the inside of the door. Some locks have only a main bolt and a latch-bolt, while others have only a main bolt. The latter types were usually used on inside doors.

At least one special type of rim lock was used in Pennsylvania, where Germanic rather than English traditions were followed in lock making. These locks have been re-garded in the past as imports from Germany, but research for this treatise has brought to light the fact that, while many of them came from that source, a few signed ones are known to have been made in America. It is also likely that a sizeable number of unsigned were made in America.

This lock differs from the rim locks pre-viously described in that the latch-bolt is moved by levers instead of knobs. They are of the three, two, and one bolt types, and have a part called a striker instead of a keeper. They are made completely of iron, with only a very few exceptions, and a few are signed by the makers. Less than a dozen signed ones are known to the writer, most of them being engraved or stamped with the name Rohrer.

There seems to have been at least two generations of this family who signed their locks.

A variation of the "Dutch" or "German" rim lock is an early latch-lock which is attached to only one plate, and the plate is mounted on the surface of the door. The latch is moved by levers or knobs on the inside and outside of the door. The unique feature of this lock is that the lever on the outside of the door is attached, or detached, by twisting it "off" or "on." The door is locked by twisting the lever off and placing it in the owner's pocket or under the door mat. This latter procedure seems to have been a universal custom and proof of the statement that "locks are only for honest people."

Another type of lock used throughout the period when locks were made by hand was the stock lock. It is said that it was called a "stock lock" because the case was made of wood and the mechanism was made of metal. The case was usually made of oak wood and the metal parts of iron; however, some of the more expensive models had brass bolts and key holes were bushed with brass fittings. The outer surface of the case were also fitted with brass inlays to make them more attractive.

A special type of stock lock was called a Bambury lock. The mechanism of the common stock lock was made completely of metal and the mechanism was inletted into the wood. The mechanism of the Bambury type was attached to the case of wood, a procedure which was less costly and less lasting.

The J & J. Patterson Lock Manufactory of Pittsburgh advertised in *Pittsburgh in 1826* by S. Jones, that they manufactured "Knob, Rim, Fine Plate, and Bambury Stock Locks, from 6 to 12 inches, also Best Norfolk Thumb Latches and Bolts." Unfortunately the writer has never seen a lock bearing the imprint of this company.

Any connoisseur of locks and lockmaking realizes that throughout the period of "handmade" locks a great many variations of door locks were made, as well as many lesser locks, such as the well known padlock. The most frequently used padlock in America seems to be the one, found principally in Pennsylvania, which is shaped like a question mark with a bar across the opening. Very few signed locks of this type have been found and none have been identified as the product of

Plate 148. *Padlock made of iron, typical of the style found in Pennsylvania. It is not definitely known where they were made. It seems likely that most of them were imported from Germany, although some could have been made in Pennsylvania. The initials "S.H." are imprinted on this one. (Kauffman Collection)* Plate 149. *Padlock, probably made by a blacksmith in New England in the early nineteenth century. The key has a slot in its end that engages a screw within the lock cylinder to release the loop of the lock. (Kauffman Collection)*

an American craftsman. It seems logical to assume that most of these locks were made in Germany and that a small number were made in Pennsylvania. Any one of these locks bearing the name Rohrer would suggest that it was made in Lebanon, Pennsylvania, where the Rohrer family worked.

The research on locks and locksmithing in America shows that many locksmiths worked here and that a large variety of locks were made. Between 1774 and 1920 at least three thousand different types were reported; obviously, many were made by county smiths who had no interest in having others know about their work. It might be pointed out that there were many secrets in all the trades and locksmithing was no exception.

The nineteenth century is frequently referred to as a period of great inventiveness in America and locksmithing certainly must be included as one of the major activities of the time. A period in the middle of the century was characterized by the "Great Lock Controversy," when every lock maker seemed to be engaged in picking his competitor's locks. An American named Hobbs bragged that he could pick any lock and made good his boast by opening all the locks made in England and exhibited at the Crystal Palace in London in 1851.

Linus Yale Sr. was one of the first men to make real progress in producing a lock that could not be "picked." His son, Linus Jr., continued this work by making locks by machinery about 1840. In 1861 and 1865 he took out patents on what is now called the Yale cylinder lock. The Yales were joined by other lock manufacturers and today the modern cylinder lock with its tumblers and fitted key seems to be about as good as a lock needs to be.

BIBLIOGRAPHY

BUEHR, WALTER. *The Story of Locks.* New York: Charles Scribner's Sons, 1953.

*Encyclopedia Perthensis; or Universal Dictionary of Knowledge.* Perth, Scotland: Printed for C. Mitchell & Co.

MOXON, JOSEPH. *Mechanick Exercises; or the Doctrine of Handy-Works.* London: Printed for D. Midwinter and Thos. Leigb, 1703.

PRICE, GEORGE. *Treatise on Fire and Thief Proof Depositories and Locks and Keys.* London, 1856.

# CHAPTER TEN

# The Gunsmith

IT IS A STRANGE PARADOX, NOT completely understood at the moment, why a man who made guns was called a gunsmith. It is true that some of the work involved in the making of a gun was done by a smith, but it is also obvious that other craftsmen such as brass-founders, woodworkers, engravers, and lockmakers were required to produce a complete gun.

It is known that, at times, a gun was made by a number of craftsmen; and that at other times, a complete gun was made by one man. It is also apparent that much forge work was required to forge and weld a gun barrel, to forge and fit the lock parts, and to forge iron mountings such as the trigger guard, the butt plates and other smaller parts. The large portion of work done on a gun by a smith suggests that the term gunsmith was evolved at a time when it was made by one man.

The derivation of the word gunsmithing is an interesting, but academic consideration in this discussion, which proposes to describe the work of the gunsmith and the interrelationship of the two trades: gunsmithing and blacksmithing. There are numerous examples of the fact that the two trades were often followed by one man. It is a well established fact that during the American Revolution, many blacksmiths were employed as gunsmiths. An important example of this practice is reported in the *Journal of the Council of the State of Virginia,* March 21, 1777:

*Official Letters of the Governors of Virginia,* Vol. I, p. 127: Mr. James Anderson this day agreed to do Blacksmith's work for the Commonwealth of Virginia at his shop in Williamsburg on the following terms for six months, and for a longer time unless he shall give the Board one month's notice of his intention to decline the Business...Mr. Anderson is to be allowed fifteen shillings per day for his own wages including Sundays, for the rent of his shop, six sets of tools, and eight vices for the Gunsmiths Business at the rate of ninety pounds per annum, he is to be allowed 6 per day for boarding each workman, for his two forges and five apprentices three pounds per month each, and if he is deprived of either of them by accident he is to supply their place with another Hand as good. He is to employ such other workmen as the public Business required on the best terms he can, and charge the country with whatever wages he pays.

Inventory made by Christoph Fogler for sunday Smith and Gun stokeing
Tools Salem the 1st Day of May 1787.

| Left column | £ | s | d |
|---|---|---|---|
| 8 Rat tail Files | | 1 | |
| 2 Plyers | | 5 | |
| 2 Hand vices | | 12 | |
| 7 Files | | 12 | |
| 1 Handsaw | | 8 | |
| 1st Steelbrass | | 5 | |
| 1 Steel blade saw | | 7 | |
| 1 Calliper | | 2 | |
| 1 Ink Stand | | | 6 |
| 1 large Vice | 1 | 10 | |
| 1 smaller Do | 2 | 5 | |
| 1 Anvil | 7 | 10 | |
| 1 Anvill horn (small) | | 1 | |
| 1 pair of Bellows | 2 | 8 | |
| 1 large Hammer | | 10 | |
| 1 small Do | | 8 | |
| 1 Stamp | | 3 | |
| 2 small Hamers | | 6 | |
| 1 Grind Stone | 1 | 16 | |
| 1 pair of Iron Shears | | 16 | |
| 1 Breast Trillis | | 10 | |
| 10 point Augres | | 5 | |
| 3 pair Tongs | | 12 | |
| 2 Work Tables with a drawer and Lock | | 12 | |
| 1 Stool or Chair | | 2 | 6 |
| 1 Fire Shovel | | 3 | |
| 1 Simulacrum | | 2 | 6 |
| 1 Repository with a foot | | 18 | |
| 1 cutting Chisel | | 1 | 6 |
| 1 anvill Do | | 1 | 8 |
| 10 Chissels | | 7 | |
| 1 pair of Pincers | | 5 | |
| 1 Compass | | 1 | |
| 8 Iron Thorns | | 3 | |
| 9 Cherries | 1 | 2 | 6 |
| 1 Handax | | 5 | |
| 10 Gun Stoks half Price | | 10 | |
| 28 Do a 18 | 1 | 16 | |
| 19 Do a 2 | 1 | 18 | |
| Wood for Ramrods | | 3 | |
| 120 Bushels of Coals a 8 | 4 | | |
| 1 Coal Shade | | 16 | |
| 1 S Jeh Club | 1 | 8 | |
| 1 Screw Blade with Augres | 1 | 16 | |
| 3 Britch Augres | | 16 | |
| Transport £ | 43 | 2 | 2 |

| Right column | £ | s | d |
|---|---|---|---|
| Brought forward £ | 43 | 2 | 2 |
| 1 Britch driver | | 6 | |
| 1 Do Blade | | 12 | |
| 1st Glue | | 1 | 0 |
| Brass | | 6 | |
| Fire Wood | | 12 | |
| Fire Stove | | 16 | |
| 1 Gage | | 3 | |
| 1 Jug with Oil | | 1 | 3 |
| 1 Do with Bone Oil | | 1 | |
| 1 Wheel | | 16 | |
| 1 Iron rod & scratcher | | 5 | |
| 8 Awles | | 3 | |
| 7 Plains | 1 | 1 | |
| 1 Whimble Augres & Bitts | 1 | 4 | |
| 1 ram rod Augre | | 6 | |
| 8 Gouges | | 8 | |
| 5 flat Chissels | | 10 | |
| 2 drawing Knifes | | 6 | |
| Carving Tools | | 16 | |
| 3 cutters | | 6 | |
| 1 Casting Ladle | | 3 | |
| 3 forging Moles | | 2 | 6 |
| 1 Powder Prove | | 6 | |
| 1 Candle Stick | | 6 | |
| 1 Cherry Turner | | 4 | |
| 1 Funnel & Cannister | | 2 | |
| Steadining Implements | | 5 | |
| Punching Irons | | 4 | |
| 1 Calliper | | 2 | 7 |
| 1 Glass with Aqua fortis | | 1 | |
| 8 Do slings | | 8 | |
| 1 Iron slings | | 1 | |
| Sundry old Iron, Loks &c | | 10 | |
| Riffle Bench with Implements | | | |
| Sand with Box, and casting Tools } | 6 | | |
| £ | 60 | 14 | 7 |

Christoph Fogler Bought this day of
Samuel Stotz for the above Price all
these Tools.

## Gun Lock Manufactory.

DANIEL SWEITZER, &co.
RESPECTFULLY inform their friends and the public in general, that they have commenced the

## Gun Lock making Business,

In the borough of Lancaster, West of the Court-house, on the street leading to Millerstown,

WHERE THEY MAKE AND REPAIR Musket Locks, Rifle do. with single and double rollers; also plain Gun and Pistol locks, in the best and neatest manner, and on reasonable terms,

WANTED,

TWO or three journeymen, who understand filing at the above busines. Good workmen will meet with good encouragement and constant employment, by applying at the factory.

N. B. Orders from a distance, post paid, will be punctually attended to.

Plate 151, above. *Gun lock manufactories were quite uncommon in American, most of such locks being imported from Birmingham, England. The Sweitzer business must not have operated a very long time because very few Sweitzer locks are found today, most of them being on Kentucky rifles made in the Lancaster, Pennsylvania area. This advertisement appeared in a Lancaster paper, August 23, 1808. (Courtesy of the Lancaster County Historical Society)*

Plate 152, right. *Floor plan of a gun shop, from the Moravian Archives in Bethlehem, Pennsylvania. The chimney near the center of the building is flanked on the left with a vestibule and on the right by the workroom for the smiths. The largest room, measuring 19 by 26 feet, is the gun stock workshop. (Courtesy of the Moravian Archives)*

Plate 150, opposite page. *Inventory of tools used by a gunsmith in Old Salem, North Carolina. Virtually all of them were made of iron and most of them have disappeared. (Courtesy of Frank Horton)*

**113 ✦ THE GUNSMITH**

It is easily understood that the urgencies of war would disturb the normal work and output of various craftsmen; however, there is evidence that the two trades of blacksmithing and gunsmithing were combined by some men also in times of peace. A trade directory of Charleston, South Carolina, for 1807, records the fact that Francis Beauchee was working at the two trades in Charleston at that time. The same directory indicates that John G. Hobrecker was working at 91 King Street as a gunsmith, but in the directories from 1809 to 1816 he is listed as a blacksmith. There are many other examples of men who simultaneously or alternately worked at the two trades.

The major portion of smith work done on a gun throughout the seventeenth and eighteenth centuries was the forging and welding of the barrel. The reason for this

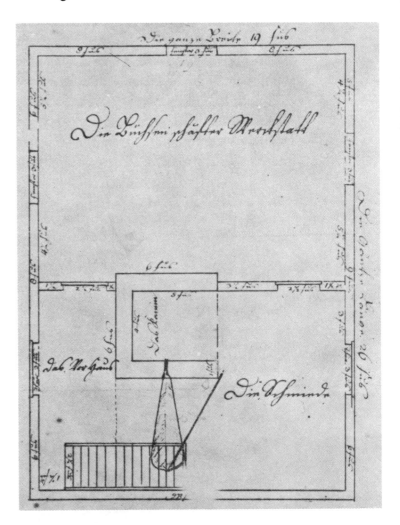

Plate 153. *The home and shop of Christoph Vogler, first of the Vogler gunsmiths in Old Salem, North Carolina. He occupied this place from 1797 to 1900, when he moved to a dam site where waterpower was available. The entrance beside the mounted gun was to his shop, beneath which his forge room was located. (Courtesy of Frank Horton)*

was that the craftsman was unable, at that time, to drill a hole through a bar of iron to make a barrel. To do the work, the common tools of the blacksmith were required with the addition of a bick-iron and a barrel anvil. The bick-iron resembled a modern ice pick but had a handle which was offset, so that it was not in line with the barrel of the gun. The barrel anvil resembled a common anvil except that the face was grooved instead of being smooth. These grooves varied in size so that barrels with different diameters could be made.

The first step in the forging of a barrel was to select a strip of soft iron, a little longer than the length of the finished barrel, and of a width that would permit rolling it into a tube with an undersize hole in it for the bore. The edges of the strip were thinned to facilitate welding and to minimize forging after the weld was made. The center section of the strip was heated first to a welding heat and then laid on one of the grooves of the anvil. The bick-iron was placed on top of the hot strip of iron and the edges were quickly folded over the bick-iron and welded. After the welding was completed, the bick-iron was removed and an adjoining section of the strip was heated to finish the welding procedure. This work was continued until the entire strip was changed into a tube.

Plates 154-5. *All metal parts of this 17th century New England fowling piece were made of iron. The trigger guard and lock are particularly attractive. (Kauffman Collection)*

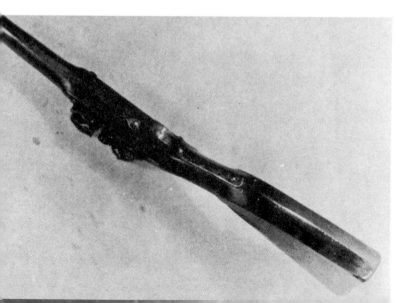

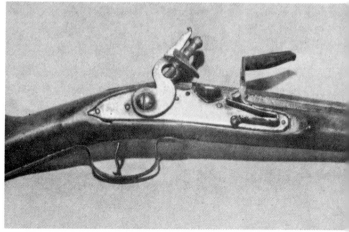

Plate 156. *The engraved signature "C. Gumpf," on the iron barrel of this Kentucky rifle, is typical of Pennsylvania gunsmiths. (Wilson Collection)*

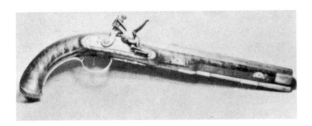

Plate 157. *Only the barrels and locks of most Kentucky pistols and rifles were made of iron. This pistol is typical of those made in Pennsylvania in the 19th century. (Kauffman Collection)*

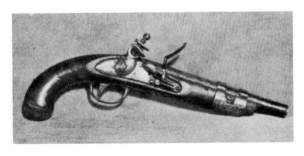

Plate 158. *All (?) parts of this S. North 1816 pistol were made of iron except the pan on the lock. It is a typical military pistol of the period. (Kauffman Collection)*

Other work remained to be done to change the tube into a gun barrel. The small hole was enlarged by long drills to the desired diameter, on a boring machine. The exterior was ground to shape or turned on a lathe and breech plug had to be fitted into the breech end of the barrel. Parts such as sights and lugs, for fastening the barrel to the stock, completed the major processes involved in the making of a barrel. Since a good blacksmith could perform all of these operations, it is easily understood why there was considerably overlapping of the two trades.

BIBLIOGRAPHY

*An Essay on Shooting.* London: T. Cadell, 1789.
GREENER, WILLIAM. *Gunnery in 1858.* London: Smith Elder & Co., 1858.
KAUFFMAN, HENRY J. *The Pennsylvania-Kentucky Rifle.* Harrisburg: The Stackpole Company, 1960.

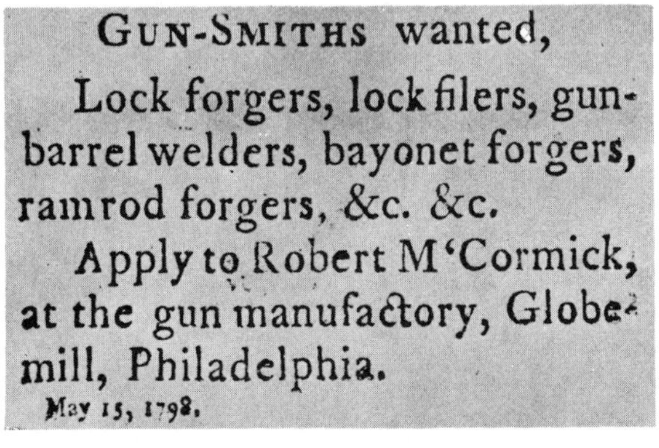

Plate 159. *Advertisement of Robert M'Cormick appearing in the Pennsylvania Herald and York General Advertiser of May 25, 1798, calling for men skilled in forging iron to work in a gun manufactory. This advertisement appearing at such an early date forecasts the high specialization that followed in most of the trades.*

**115 ✦ THE GUNSMITH**

GUN-SMITHS wanted, Lock forgers, lock filers, gun-barrel welders, bayonet forgers, ramrod forgers, &c. &c.

Apply to Robert M'Cormick, at the gun manufactory, Globe mill, Philadelphia.

May 15, 1798,

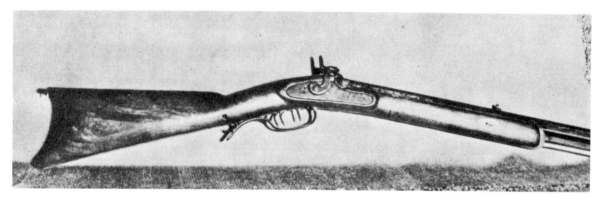

Plate 160. *Iron was used for all the metal parts of this Indian "trade" rifle, made in mid-19th century by J. Henry at Boulton, Pennsylvania. (Kauffman Collection)*

Plate 161. *Unusual iron bullet extractor, probably for use in the barrel of a pistol. The workmanship is of very high quality. Such tools made entirely of iron are very rare. (Courtesy of Harold L. Peterson)*

Plate 162. *A very late flint lock of iron (with hammer cap and screw missing), bearing the imprint of P.A. & S. Small. The Small Company was in the hardware business in York, Pennsylvania, and a number of their locks are found on Kentucky rifles. (Kauffman Collection)*

Plate 163. *The metal parts of many military arms were made entirely of iron. On this 1819 Harpers Ferry musket iron was used except for the pan on the lock, made of brass. (Kauffman Collection)*

# CHAPTER ELEVEN

# The Nailer

THE TRADE OF NAIL MAKING HAS received little recognition in the history of handicrafts in metal; however, a great many men were engaged in the trade and they produced a large variety of nails. Three types of craftsmen made nails. The general blacksmith made them as an adjunct to his trade when there was a lull in business or when a customer needed a quantity for a particular project. If there were an unusual demand for nails at a particular time or place, the blacksmith might hire a man who did nothing but make nails. Such men probably lacked the imagination required of a blacksmith or were without the business ability to manage a blacksmithing business. The third group were farmers who had small forges on their farms and made nails to augment the meager income they received from their crops.

A statement by Mr. Ames, quoted in the *History of America Manufactures* by Bishop, Philadelphia, 1861, describes nail making on the farm as follows:

This manufacture, with very little encouragement, has grown up remarkable. It has become common for the country people in Massachusetts to erect small forges in their chimney-corners, and in the winter evenings when little other work can be done, great quantities of nails were made by children. These people take the rod of iron from the merchant and return him nails; and, in consequence of this easy mode of barter, the manufacture is prodigiously great. The advantages are not exclusively in the hands of the people of Massachusetts. The business might be pursued in a similar manner in every state exerting equal industry.

Nails were made by hand over a long period of time and it is interesting to note that their shape and the method of making them changed very little until they were made by machine. Albert Sonn tells in his *Early American Wrought Iron* that a nail found on the Roman Forum would differ little from one found on Boston Common a thousand years later.

Dr. H. C. Mercer explains how a nail was made by hand in his article, "The Dating of Old Houses":

The following Articles manufactured at

*Delaware Works.*

Spike and nail rods of different fizes
Sheet iron
Phaeton and chair tire
Bands for burr millftones, broad and narrow
Nails 8d, 10d, 12d, 20d and 30d, flat and fharp points
Deck, drawing, and fheathing nails
Flooring brads 12d and 20d
Curry combs.

*WANTED at faid WORKS,*

APPRENTICES from ten to fourteen years of age, to learn the Nailing and Smith's bufinefs. The boys will be placed under the direction of *fober*, induftrious workmen, and will be fuitably cloathed and fed during their apprenticefhip; and inftructed in reading, writing and arithmetic; and when of age will each receive one new fuit of cloaths, and fifteen dollars in money, for the purpofe of furnifhing themfelves with a fet of tools.

A Perfon that has been ufed to work under a Tilt Hammer, will, if a good hand, meet with encouragement by applying to Samuel Ogden, at Delaware Works, or to Ifaac Hazlehurft & Co.

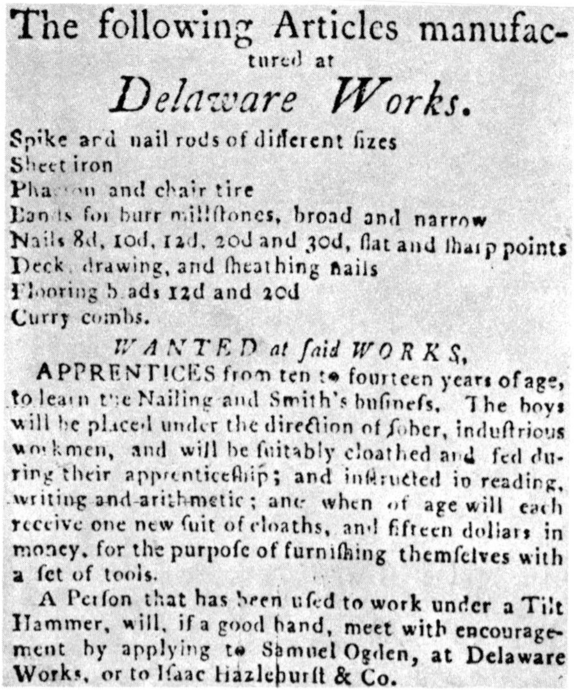

Plate 164. *Advertisement of the Delaware Works appearing in the Pennsylvania Packet and Daily Advertiser of August 1, 1787. Note that nails were among the products manufactured. (Courtesy of the Historical Society of Pennsylvania)*

The wrought-iron nail was made from rectangular strips of malleable iron, several feet long and about a quarter inch thick called nail rods, which were furnished to the blacksmith or nailer, who holding one in his hand, heated its end in the forge, and then on the anvil, pointed it with a hammer on four sides. Next he partly cut it above the point on the 'hardy' with a hammer blow, and then, inserting the hot point in the swage hole, he broke off the rod and hammered the projecting end so as to spread it around the top of the hole; after which, the cooling shrunken nail was easily knocked out of the orifice.

Plate 165. *Various shapes of nails made by blacksmiths and nailers in the 18th and 19th centuries. It is evident that the function of the nail had a great influence on its shape and size.* From left to right, first group: *L-headed rafter spikes. Blunt-ended type was driven through mortise and tenon joint as a pin.* Second group: *Forged L-headed nails. Small ones used for trim, mouldings, and picture frames.* Third group: *T-headed forged nails used for trim and floors. Rose*

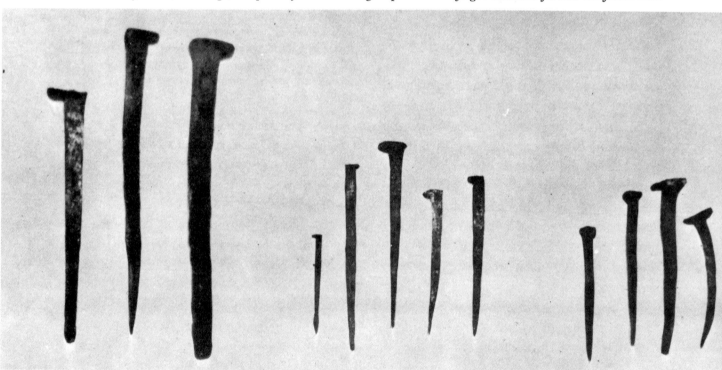

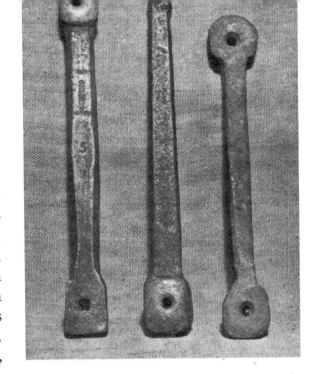

Many types of nails were made; as a matter of fact, twenty-two different ones are described in *The City and Country Purchaser, and Builder's Dictionary* by Richard Neve, London, 1726. These types were used in architecture and many others must have been made for other uses. The Neve list includes the following types: back and bottom, clamp, clasp, strong, clench, clout, deck,

heads were formed first and then two or four sides were flattened down against the shank. Fourth group: *Bellows nails.* Fifth group: *Rose-headed forged nails with chisel point.* Sixth group: *Rose-headed forged nails with pointed ends.* Small ones were used for lath, larger ones for clinching if needed. Seventh group: *Chisel-pointed spikes. (Courtesy of Donald Streeter)*

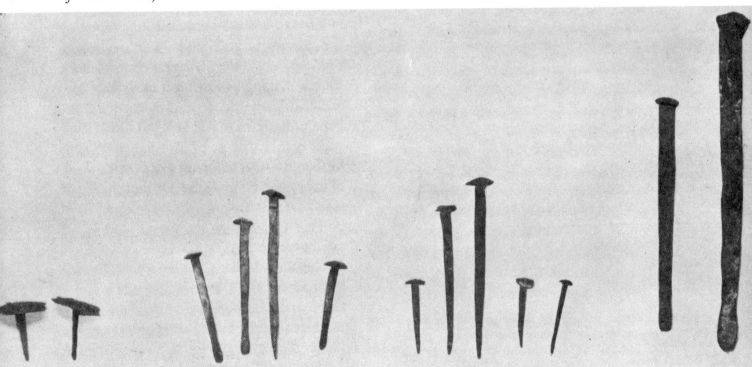

dog, flatpoint, jobent, lead, port, pound, ribbing, rose, round heat, scupper, sharp, sheathing, square and tacks. At least one of these nails was made in thirty sizes, and most were made in at least four to six sizes. Obviously, all of them were made for some special purpose and at least one type was tin plated to improve its appearance and preserve it from rust and final disintegration.

The demand for nails was so great at the end of the eighteenth century that nail factories were established to produce large quantities by hand. The following advertisement appeared in the *New York Journal and Patriotic Record* on April 12, 1791:

TO BE SOLD Or Exchanged for Property in the Country, On Advantageous Terms.

THAT well known nail Manufactory and Smith Works, No. 22 Cherry Street, now in compleat repair with tools and implements sufficient to employ 28 workmen—These works are so well known and established, that the proprietor may, with property assert that his nails have a more universal circulation than any others manufactured in America. Any person willing to purchase the above works, and employ the hands now at work, will be enabled to keep up the credit of this manufactory as is now established. And the subscriber assures the public that the business bears a more flattering prospect than it ever had since its commencement.

As he wishes to enter in a line of business more retired is his only motive for disposing of the same. For further particulars apply to the subscriber on the premises.

JACOB FOSTER

Although it is known that nails were made by hand in Lancaster County, Pennsylvania, as late as 1900, the Industrial Revolution of the late eighteenth and early nineteenth centuries led to the invention of machinery for the making of nails. It is likely that Mr. Foster foresaw the impending change from hand production to machine production and was eager to dispose of his hand-producing facility. There is no doubt that Foster's manufactory had no machines for the making of nails; for if it had, he certainly would have pointed out such an important asset in his sale advertisement.

There is substantial evidence that the embryo nation, the United States, was a leader in the producing of nails by machine. These machines were adapted to steam, water, or horse power and were regarded even in England as devices of uncommon merit.

Plate 168. *Advertisement for horse nails appearing in the Burlington (Iowa) Hawk-Eye of February 7, 1877. It appears that his machine-made nails had a hand-made quality.*

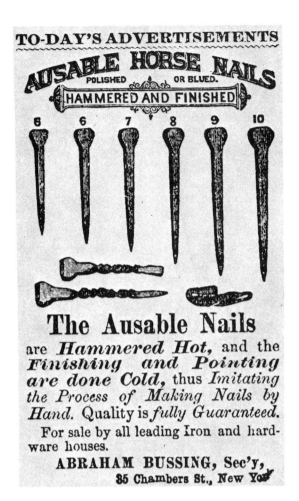

Between 1790 and September, 1825, the manufacturing of nails was the subject of 120 patents. It is reported that after the domestic demands were met, great quantities were exported.

An advertisement in a Philadelphia, Pennsylvania, *Pocket Newspaper* shows the eagerness of one nail maker to tell about the invention and to sell its products.

### HARRISBURG
#### Nail Manufactory

The subscriber respectfully informs the citizens of Pennsylvania, that he carries on the Nail Factory at Harrisburg by cutting, without the usual mode of drawing (being the invention of his late father David Folsome) where Nails and Sprigs, of any kind, from Shingle down to 2d sprigs, may be had, either by the single pound or quantity, much cheaper than imported nails. He is much flattered with the encouragement he has hitherto had in the prosecution of this business, and he hopes a continuance of Public Favor. Orders from store keepers and others who may want by quantity, will be duly attended to, and the utmost care and punctuality observed.

WILLIAM J. FOLSOME

The usual arguments ensued in the press and among craftsmen concerning the relative merits of machine-made versus hand-made nails. A statement from Dr. Ure's *Dictionary of Arts, Manufactures, and Mines,* New York, 1856, comments forcibly on this matter, as follows:

For sheathing and drawing cut (manufactured) nails are full as good as wrought nails; only in one respect are the best wrought nails a little superior to cut anils, and that is where it is necessary they should be clinched.

It is probable that prejudice against the new and a sympathy for the old caused hand-wrought nails to be used for many years after machine-made nails were available. It is also likely that some people said more for the old nail to perpetuate its use rather than succumb to using the new, cheap, fashionable nails. At least it is apparent that a century of time was required to completely cast the old aside.

### BIBLIOGRAPHY
BISHOP, LEANDER J. *A History of American Manufacture from 1608 to 1860.* Philadelphia: Edward Young & Co., 1861.

MERCER, HENRY C. *The Dating of Old Houses. Boston: Old-Time New England.* Bulletin of the Society for the Preservation of New England Antiquities, April, 1924.

NEVE, RICHARD. *The City and Country Purchaser and Builder's Dictionary; or the Compleat Builders Guide.* London: Printed for D. Browne and Ch. Rivington, 1726.

SONN, ALBERT. *Early American Wrought Iron.* 3 vols. New York: Charles Scribner's Sons, 1928.

URE, ANDREW. *A Dictionary of Arts, Manufactures, and Mines; containing a Clear Exposition of their Principles and Practice.* 2 vol. New York: D. Appleton and Company, 1856.

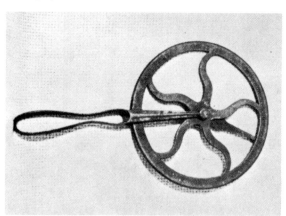

Plate 169. *Wheel-race or traveler, for determing the circumference of a wheel, made of cast iron by Willy & Russel Manufacturing Company, Greenfield, Massachusetts. (Courtesy of Reginald French)*

Plate 170. *The small wheel of this sturdy wheelbarrow, with its iron rim, was constructed in the same manner as those used on large wagons. (Courtesy of Wood's Antiques)*

Plate 171. *Wheel from a Pennsylvania farm wagon of the 19th century. Although all evidence of its preserving paint have disappeared, it is still strong and sturdy. (Courtesy of Wood's Antiques)*

# CHAPTER TWELVE

# The Wheelwright

IT IS NOT KNOWN WHEN THE FIRST wagons, or vehicles with wheels, were made in America; but it seems reasonable to presume from a knowledge about contemporary objects that there was a sizeable production here in the first half of the eighteenth century. It is probable that many of the earliest vehicles were two-wheeled carts similar to the ones used in Europe at that time. Extremely few, if any, of this early type of cart have survived for comparison and study. It is likely that the four-wheeled wagons were also influenced by European styles with some adaptations to the terrain and function of the wagon in America.

It is clearly pointed out in *The English Farm Wagon* by F. Gerant Jenkins, Reading, 1961, that two crafts were involved in the making and repairing of wagons in Europe. One was a man who is called a general blacksmith, in this survey, and the other was called a wheelwright. Sometimes one man followed both trades; sometimes two men followed the two separate trades but worked together;

and sometimes a wheelwright worked at this trade alone.

A man called a "wright" is known as an artificer or handcraftsman, and one might logically conclude that a wheelwright made wheels. The Oxford English Dictionary suggests a wider application of the word wheelwright in its definition which follows: "A man who makes wheels and wheeled vehicles."

It is evident from the definition of the wheelwright that his work generally included the making of a complete wagon; however, in this survey, only his work in iron will be considered. The Shirley Martin survey of craftsmen working in Bucks County, Pennsylvania from 1750 to 1800 focuses attention on the fact that the trade of wheelwright was widely followed in rural areas. Of the one hundred and forty-five craftsmen in working metals at that time, one hundred and four were blacksmiths and thirty-four were wheelwrights. The need for wagons was great in the newly settled rural areas of Pennsylvania and there were obviously craftsmen located there to meet the demand. An interesting advertisement in *Kline's Carlisle Gazette,* September 17, 1800, indicates the need for apprentices at that time.

WANTED. AN APPRENTICE TO THE WAGON-MAKING BUSINESS. A BOY from 14 to 16 years of age. Fur further details apply to PHILLIP GROVE, Wagon-maker in Carlisle.

This advertisement suggests that wagon making was also an important trade on the Pennsylvania frontier. Carlisle was then a small country village located on the route from Philadelphia to Fort Pitt. The wagon-making industry could well have been a flourishing business at such a critical point on that important trade route.

The actual techniques used by wagon makers in America is a subject that has not been thoroughly investigated; however, the migration of European craftsmen to America suggests that American techniques were generally similar to those followed in Europe. This theory is substantiated by the fact that the style of American wagons was obviously adapted from European styles, that craftsmen were constantly migrating to America from Europe, and there is evidence of American craftsmen using techniques of European origin in trades such as coppersmithing, blacksmithing, silversmithing, and others.

The extensive survey of *The English Farm Wagon* by F. Gerald Jenkins, Reading, 1961, reports the way much of the smith work was

Plates 172-3. *Conestoga wagons displayed at the Pennsylvania State Farm Museum in Lanis Valley. Originally all had roofs of homespun. The bodies were painted blue and the undercarriages an orange-red. When freshly painted they were very attractive. (Courtesy of the Pennsylvania Historical and Museum Commission)*

Plate 174. *Carriage factory at Goodville, Lancaster County, Pennsylvania. The ramp was used in moving carriages between the first and second floors. Note the charming bell tower on the roof.* (Kauffman photo)

done in England from the start of production there until the beginning of the twentieth century. The major work of the smith was concerned with the making of the iron tire for the wheels. Other work was connected with the making of body braces, axle bearings, hub bands, and hub inserts called boxes.

In the making of an iron tire, the work of the smith might be logically prefaced by an explanation of the various parts of a wheel. The central part of the wheel was called a hub, a knave, or a stock, and it was made of elm wood. An even number of spokes radiated from the center to the outer portion of the wheel which were made of split-oak. The felloes were curved portions of wood forming a circular rim for the wheel. The various parts of the wheel were bound together by a hoop of heavy metal called a tire, or by a series of short crescent-shaped pieces of iron called strakes.

The first procedure in making a tire was to secure a strip of metal a little wider than the rim of the wheel to be tired. The circumference of the wheel was measured by a disc

of wood about ten inches in diameter, called a "traveller." The disc was attached to a handle which permitted the disc to freely rotate as it was pushed around the outer surface of the wheel. The number of revolutions it traveled around the wheel were noted, and it was then pushed an equal distance on the iron for the tire. The tire had to be made oversize or the shrinking tire would bind the wheel too tightly. Provision had to be made also for the overlapping portion of the tire where the welded joint was made.

The first operation in the forming of a tire was called scarfing. A scarf was a tapered section on each end of the strip so that when the weld was made, the welded (and overlapped) portion would be only as thick as the balance of the tire. A hole was punched in the middle of each scarf for use in holding the ends in place during the welding process. After the strip of iron was shaped into a circle by hand, or later by a tire bender, the joint was placed in the fire and raised to a welding heat. When the exterior surface of the iron became pasty, it was forced together with a hammer and the joint was "worked" until the joint could not be detected. The final work at the forge was to reheat the tire

and punch a number of holes through it so that the tire could be fastened to the rim with nails.

An open fire of wood shavings and small sticks was made in the yard to fit the circumference of the wheel. Later wheelwrights had a vertical oven built of bricks for heating a number of tires at one time. The untired wheel was fastened to a horizontal plate to keep it in place while the tire was applied. After the tire was heated to a red heat, two or three men lifted the tire from the fire with long tongs and dropped it on the ground to break away the loose oxidation caused by the fire. The same men then raised the tire over the wheel, dropped it over the rim, and hammered it in place. The shrinking, cooling tire tightly bound the loose component parts of the wheel into one strong, integrated unit. Water was then poured on the tire to prevent further burning of the wooden rim.

After complete cooling, the wheel was mounted on a larger wheel which rotated like the headstock of a lathe. The rough and burned portions of the wheel were removed as it was rotated, and final preparations were made for painting it.

In the earliest times, wheels were bound by strakes, and despite the fact that a tire was a better device for the outer part of the wheel, strakes continued to be used. This procedure was followed because if part of a wheel needed repairs, only a portion of the

Plate 175. *Wheel used on a farm wagon in Pennsylvania, probably in the 19th century, showing how various bands of metal were used in the construction of a hub made principally of wood. (Courtesy of Wood's Antiques)*

outer covering could be easily removed, a small section, or strake was easier to heat and shape than a large tire, and all the repair operations could be performed by a farmer instead of taking the tire to a wheelwright. Sometimes strakes were mounted over the tire to prevent abnormal wear on a portion of the tire and eventual replacement.

The final metalwork done on the wheel was to fit the bands to the exterior of the hub and to install a box inside the hub. A box consisted of two metal bushings placed within the wooden hub to prevent wear on the wood. The earliest method was to fix two cast iron cylinders in the hub, one in each end. These boxes rotated on metal plates inserted on the top and bottom surface of the wooden axles. These plates were called

skeins. On later iron axles, a cast iron fitting lined the entire interior of the hub. The collar was a raised projection on the iron axle, forming the bearing against which the hub box rotated.

One of the outstanding achievements of the American wheelwright was the making of the ironwork for Conestoga wagons. This wagon was used principally by the German settlers who lived around Lancaster, Pennsylvania. Its name was taken from the Conestoga Creek which flowed through one of the richest agricultural areas in the New World. The design of the wagon is regarded by many people as unique to America, but it obviously had many details found on European farm wagons. The "boat" shape of the body and the hemp cover for the top are possibly unique features of the Pennsylvania wagon.

The wheels for the Conestoga wagon were tall, wide, and heavy to comfortably travel over the rough terrain of the newly opened country. The hub for a rear wheel was twenty inches long, it had a circumference of thirty-eight inches, and it had sixteen spokes. The tire was approximately five feet in diameter and three and one-half inches wide. The front wheels were approximately forty-two inches in diameter and other specifications were properly scaled to the size of the wheel. The wheels and the under-

carriage were painted red, the body blue, and the hemp cover soon bleached to a pure white.

Although the work of the wheelwright was of great importance in the making of tires for wheels of the Conestoga wagons, this work has been virtually unnoticed when compared with the interest in the decorative iron-work used on the other parts of the wagon. It is likely that the wheelwright usually made all of the ironwork for the wagon, but there is evidence that there were some specialists in the "ironing of a wagon." This hypothesis is supported by an advertisement from *Kline's Carlisle Gazette,* March 26, 1794.

WANTED IMMEDIATELY
TWO apprentices to the Black Smith and Sickle-making Business. Likewise, two journeymen that understand the ironing of wagons and country business as well, such will find good encouragement by applying to the subscriber, living in Shippensburg, near the sign of the bear.
THOMAS HIBBEN
Shippensburg, March 26, 1794

The work of "ironing the wagon" includes the making of parts such as chains, hounds bands, brake levers, body braces, stay-chain hooks, brake shoes, axe hangers, and decorative parts for the tool boxes. Axe hangers were cleverly forged and beautifully decorated with geometric patterns or designs from nature. The fish was a favorite pattern for many craftsmen. Chains made of intricately twisted links were used on a

Plate 178. *Carriages at a Mennonite Church near Morgantown, Pennsylvania. Even today wheelwrights are still busy in Lancaster County, Pennsylvania. (Kauffman photo)*

**EARLY AMERICAN IRONWARE ✦ 128**

Plate 179. *Iron fittings used on Conestoga wagons. (Courtesy Pennsylvania Historical & Museum Commission)*

number of the wagon parts, and each smith seems to have lavished unusual effort in the forging and shaping of the links. Coiled snakes with raised heads were another design used on iron parts of the wagon and its fittings. The coiled snake can definitely be traced to earlier use in Europe.

All of the ironwork on the Conestoga wagon was well wrought and interesting, but the smith reached the zenith of his craft in the "ironing" of the tool box. The box was made of wood and was mounted on the left side of the wagon where it was easily accessible in times of emergency. It contained accessories such as wire, nails, pinchers, hammers, gloves, etc. The boxes varied according to the size of the wagon to which they were attached. They were generally about twelve to fifteen inches long, possibly ten to twelve inches wide, and about eighteen to twenty inches deep. The back of the box was flat and it was attached to the

wagon bed with iron bands. The front of the box was triangular in shape; the lid slanting away from the bed at a thirty degree angle.

The lid was attached to the body by two staples which formed part of the hinges. The highly ornamented hinges were beautifully displayed on the slanting lid, and the finials of the hinges usually matched the finial on the hasp. Motifs such as hearts and tulips were favorites of the smiths to decorate their products. Mythical beliefs are often attached to the various forms used by the smiths, but these are discredited by most authorities who have made a study of the period in which they were used. It seems safe to say that no product of the American smith is more eagerly sought today than a beautifully ornamented tool box from a Conestoga wagon.

It is interesting to note that despite the fact that vehicles were made in factories in the nineteenth century, the wheelwright was never completely forced out of business. By using "factory made" axles and springs, he continued to fabricate vehicles as he had done in the past.

As a matter of fact, some wheelwrights have wagon and buggy shops in Lancaster County, Pennsylvania, today. They are largely patronized by the Amish who believe that a modern internal combustion motor is a device of the Devil. All their vehicles are "horse drawn" and Amish buggies are frequently seen on the streets of villages such as New Holland, Blue Ball, and Intercourse.

There are probably some wheelwrights working in other rural areas of America, but their days are obviously numbered, and they will soon completely disappear from the countryside. The demands for their trade were high, and it is obvious that many of them produced very creditable products.

BIBLIOGRAPHY

JENKINS, GERANT J. *The English Farm Wagon, Origins and Structure.* Lingfield, Surrey, England: Oakwood Press for the University of Reading, 1961.

OMWAKE, JOHN. *Conestoga Six Horse Bell Team, 1750-1850.* Cincinnati: Ebbert & Richardson Co., 1930.

Plate 180. *Ironwork on the lid of a Conestoga wagon tool box, showing unusually fine craftsmanship in its symmetry and simplicity. (Courtesy of the Philadelphia Museum of Art)*

# CHAPTER THIRTEEN

# The Tinsmith

LITTLE ATTENTION HAS BEEN given to the material with which the tinsmith worked, and in most surveys it is simply stated that he worked in tin or, more correctly, tin plate. At no time in the history of handicrafts has the tinsmith been described as a craftsman who worked in iron. The fallacy of the concept that the tinsmith worked in tin can be easily traced to certain definitions of tin, like the one found in the late eighteenth century *Encyclopedia Perthensis,* which defines this metal as "a thin sheet of iron covered with tin." A similar, and misleading, definition appears in the nineteenth century *American Dictionary of the English Language,* Springfield, Massachusetts, 1848, which defines tin as "thin plates of iron covered with tin." Both of these definitions emphasize the fact that the sheet of iron was thin but make no comment on the thickness of the coating of tin. The fact is that, of the total thickness of tin plate, possibly ninety percent was iron and ten per cent tin.

A close scrutiny reveals tin to be a very soft, silvery-white, malleable, and easily soldered metal. Pure tin closely resembles pewter in its physical qualities because pewter is composed for the most part of tin. The close resemblance of these two metals is confirmed in the German language, where the word "zinn" is used for both. It is well-known that tin has neither the strength nor the rigidity required for daily household use and, because of its low melting point, utensils made of it may not be used on a stove.

There was a metal called "block tin" from which articles were made in the eighteenth and nineteenth centuries; it is defined in *The American Dictionary of the English Language* as "tin as it comes in blocks from the foundry." It was obviously pure tin and objects made of it were usually formed by foundry methods. It is interesting to note that Longworth's *Dictionary of New York City* for 1831-32 lists Boardman and Hart as craftsmen in block tin and pewter.

Another metal used by some tinsmiths, principally in the eighteenth century, was sheet-iron. This uncoated sheet metal was

Plate 181. *Tin document box, possibly of the late 18th century, having a green background. This color and the style of decoration are unique. (Kauffman Collection)*

The fact that the advertiser is asking for tinmen suggests that a scarcity of sheet iron workers existed at that time. Such an hypothesis is supported by entries in trade directories, for they contain few references to craftsmen called sheet iron workers.

Because of the uncertainty that exists concerning the nature of tin plate, some atten-

utilized to make industrial equipment and camp equipment for the military. Many of the fine weather vanes on barns and public buildings were made of sheet iron. An advertisement in the *New York Gazette,* August 12, 1776, throws some light on the subject:

Tin men wanted. Very good encouragement will be given to fifteen or twenty men, who understand the working of flat-iron into kettles, if they apply to Samuel Ogden, at Booneton, in Morris County, New Jersey; who hath rod and sheet iron of all sizes to dispose of. Apply to Josiah Shippey, at Mr. Isaac Roosevelt's in New York.

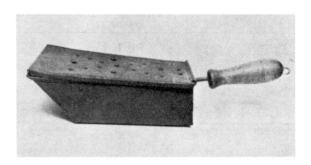

Plate 182. *Fire carrier used to convey hot coals from one fireplace to another. The metal is not coated with tin and the joints are not soldered. The holes were strictly for ventilation. (Kauffman Collection)*

tion might be given to its qualities and methods of production. It is interesting to note that no sizeable quantity of this material was produced in America until late in the nineteenth century and that, although the methods of producing it changed, the character of the metal remained the same.

The following statement from *Pontypool*

Plate 183. *The local tinsmith made many objects used on the farm. This milk bucket with a number of seams indicates that the tinsmith either had small pieces of tin with which to work or simply utilized scrap pieces when he made this one. Regardless of the joinery, they did attempt to decorate such buckets with a bead near the center and another at the top. (Kauffman Collection)*

Plate 184. *Weather vane of sheet iron used on a girl's private school in York, Pennsylvania in the 19th century, possibly made by Fisher who advertised his making of sheet iron objects. (Courtesy of the York County Historical Society)*

*and Usk Japanned Ware*, Newport, England, furnishes some insight into the early manufacture of tin plate in Europe:

From the date of its first introduction (1550) until about 1620, the melting of tin plates was maintained exclusively in Bohemia, whence they were supplied to the whole of Europe (packed in small barrels holding about 450 sheets which weighed about 2 cwts.), and were shipped down the river Elbe, via Hamburg, to England in rapidly increasing quantities: without doubt information relating to all manufacturing operations in Bohemia was held as secretly as possible.

Since there was in England an abundance of iron ore and refining facilities, and a surplus of tin from the mines of Cornwall, a group of ironmasters there became interested in producing tin plate. Eleven of them created a fund to pay the expenses of three men, who were to go to Germany, pirate the details of production, and bring them back to England. From 1665 to 1667. these men

toured the areas where tin plate was made and, after returning to England, assisted in the first successful production of tin plate in the British Isles. About 1670, tests of the plate were made by the London tinsmiths, Harrison and Lydiate, who pronounced the manufacture successful in every respect.

At first the operations in the production of tin plate were tedious and slow. The sheet had to be hammered with great skill from bar stock with a tilt hammer. The cleaning, or pickling, of the sheet was a desperate

Plate 185. *Weather vane of sheet iron from Hagerstown, Maryland, called "Little Heiskell." This charming figure doubtless was repulsing invaders from his native city. (On permanent loan from the Mayor and Council of Hagerstown to the Washington County Historical Society)*

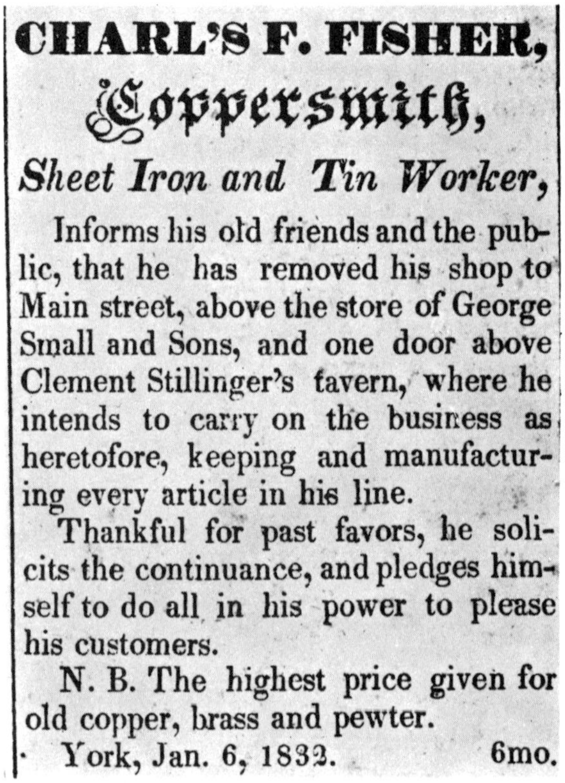

## CHARL'S F. FISHER,
### 𝕮𝖔𝖕𝖕𝖊𝖗𝖘𝖒𝖎𝖙𝖍,
### Sheet Iron and Tin Worker,

Informs his old friends and the public, that he has removed his shop to Main street, above the store of George Small and Sons, and one door above Clement Stillinger's tavern, where he intends to carry on the business as heretofore, keeping and manufacturing every article in his line.

Thankful for past favors, he solicits the continuance, and pledges himself to do all in his power to please his customers.

N. B. The highest price given for old copper, brass and pewter.

York, Jan. 6, 1832.          6mo.

affair, usually carried on underground in a very hot room with sealed doors. It had been learned in Germany that sour fermented rye cereal, to which small amounts of sal-ammoniac were added, acted as a detergent in cleaning the surfaces of the sheet metal. In these underground areas large vats were filled with bruised rye cereal. Fires were maintained under the vats; workers entered the rooms a few times daily to turn the iron sheets or to transfer them from one vat to another. After three days of soaking, they were removed and scoured by women, using fine abrasive sand.

Plate 186. *Early 19th century advertisement from a York Pennsylvania newspaper. It should be noted that Fishe, indicated he worked in sheet iron as well copper and tin. Few tradesmen indicated in their advertisements that they worked in sheet iron. (Courtesy of the York County Historical Society)*

After a very thorough cleaning, the sheets were placed in large cast-iron cauldrons containing molten tin. Fires were kept going under the cauldrons and a half-ton of tin was melted at a time. A thick layer of tallow floated on top to reduce oxidation. After the molten tin had been stirred about thirty to forty minutes, single sheets of coated iron were removed with a pair of tongs. After draining and cooling, they were redipped to provide a thicker coating of tin on the sheet iron. After the second dipping, they were rubbed dry and bright by girls, using sawdust, oatmeal, or moss.

In 1780 it was found that diluted hydrochloric acid was excellent for cleaning the scale from the sheet iron, and in 1790 an improved rolling technique brought the production of tin plate to a high level. The product became cheaper and could be easily obtained from ironmongers or hardware merchants in all the American cities on the Atlantic seaboard.

It seems evident from the foregoing discussion that tin plate had some of the qualities of both iron and tin. Like iron, it was rigid, strong, and it held its shape after hammering

Plate 187. *Tin nursing bottles from Pennsylvania, each holding only a few ounces of liquid. One has a forward spout and the other a side spout. (Kauffman Collection)*

or bending. Like tin, it was white, rustproof, and could be soldered easily. The large quantity of iron used in the manufacture of tin plate confirms the fact that the artisan was essentially a worker in iron.

It is evident from research, although not from surviving pieces, that a wide range of tinware, manufactured in England, was shipped to America in the seventeenth century. An interesting assortment of these products is recorded in a legal suit between John Caxy, a London merchant, and Joseph Mallenson, a Boston merchant who was unable to pay for the consignment sent to him in 1764. The list follows:

One Large hh No 3 q of Tinnerie Ware Viz
6 Lathorns
2 large fish kettles and plate
2 small ditto
6 large Pastry pans
6 small ditto
3 setts kettles

3 doz. pocket graders
1 doz. large square pudding pans
1 doz. ditto small
6 pairs of Snuffers and Pans
6 hanging candlesticks
2 doz. large Porringers
3 doz. middle ditto
2 doz. small ditto
6 large funnels
2 doz. quart ditto
1 doz. large Sauce pans
2 doz. Flower boxes
2 doz. pepper boxes
4 Large Dripping pans
1 doz. large round pudding pans
1 doz. candlesticks
6 Planish Candlesticks

Plate 189. *Ordinary tin basin typical of those used throughout Pennsylvania in the late 19th and early 20th centuries, probably made by local tinsmiths, or possibly manufactured in Baltimore or Philadelphia. (Kauffman Collection)*

1 doz. casting ladles
1 doz. bread graters
1 doz. tinder boxes
8 Candle boxes
6 round fish plates
6 Cullendars
1 doz. half pint pots
A large Casque

This extensive listing of tinware indicates that tin articles were readily available and widely used in the New World. It suggests that repairmen were needed and that, in some instances, they might have fabricated a few new pieces from some that had been discarded or from new tin plate. All the pieces were formed by hand; this does not imply that the surfaces were uneven or that there was indifferent fitting on the corners. It can be safely stated that, although later machine fabrication did increase production, there was no noticeable improvement in the quality of the product.

The history of tinsmithing in America in the eighteenth century is on more certain ground. It is a most fortunate circumstance that the account book of America's first known tinsmith, Shem Drowne, has been preserved in the archives of the American Antiquarian Society. The earliest entries (1720) report that he made or repaired lan-

terns, candlemolds, trays, and candlestikcs. Drowne's real claim to fame, in addition to his being our earliest known tinsmith, lies in the fact that he made a number of weather vanes of sheet copper—the Indian vane for Province House, a chanticleer for Hanover Street Church, and a grasshopper for Faneuil Hall, all of Boston, Massachusetts. When the grasshopper was repaired by Shem's son, Thomas, he placed within the body of the vane the following statement: "Shem Drown mad itt, May 25, 1742."

Although Bishop states in his *History of American Manufactures* that the Pattison brothers of Berlin, Connecticut were the first tinsmiths in America, it is now apparent that research has proved this statement to be inaccurate. Edward Pattison was born in 1730 and reached the height of his production about 1770. The founder of the tin business in Berlin died in 1787, after which time the operation of the tin factory was carried on by his two sons, Edward and Shubael, throughout the first quarter of the nineteenth century.

Another important center of tin production was located at Stevens Plains, Maine, where it was begun by Zachariah Stevens, a name well-known to all tin lovers because of his major role in the book, *Early American Decoration*, by his descendant, Esther Stevens Brazier. Various craftsmen of note came to Stevens Plains; in 1832 it was reported that an annual business of $27,000 was transacted there. Other noteworthy figures in the tin world of the nineteenth century include the

Plate 190. *Decorated tin document box, probably from New England, typical of the 19th century. (Kauffman Collection)*

**EARLY AMERICAN IRONWARE ✦ 136**

Butlers of Greenville, New York, and Oliver Filley of Bloomfield, Connecticut.

These men, all outstanding craftsmen, dominated the tinware production of their day; however, the onrushing Industrial Revolution was soon to sweep them from their work benches to a desk in the "front-office." Eli Whitney had invented a way to increase the production of guns, textile operations were "up," and the tinshop was slowly growing from a shop to a factory. Instead of one or two men laboriously fashioning a few objects by hand, many men were now producing a variety of products by hand-operated machines.

It has been determined, from a study of the records of the United States Patent Office, that a number of men were engaged in the business of inventing new machinery for the tin trade. On May 9, 1814, a patent was issued to David Noble of Philadelphia, for an undescribed machine for the manufacturing of objects from tin plate. A patent for

Plate 192. *Tin sconce for a single candle. Sconces usually were not painted because of the heat of the flame. This one has attractive flutes and beads made on a hand-operated machine. (Courtesy of The Metropolitan Museum of Art)*

**137 ✦ THE TINSMITH**

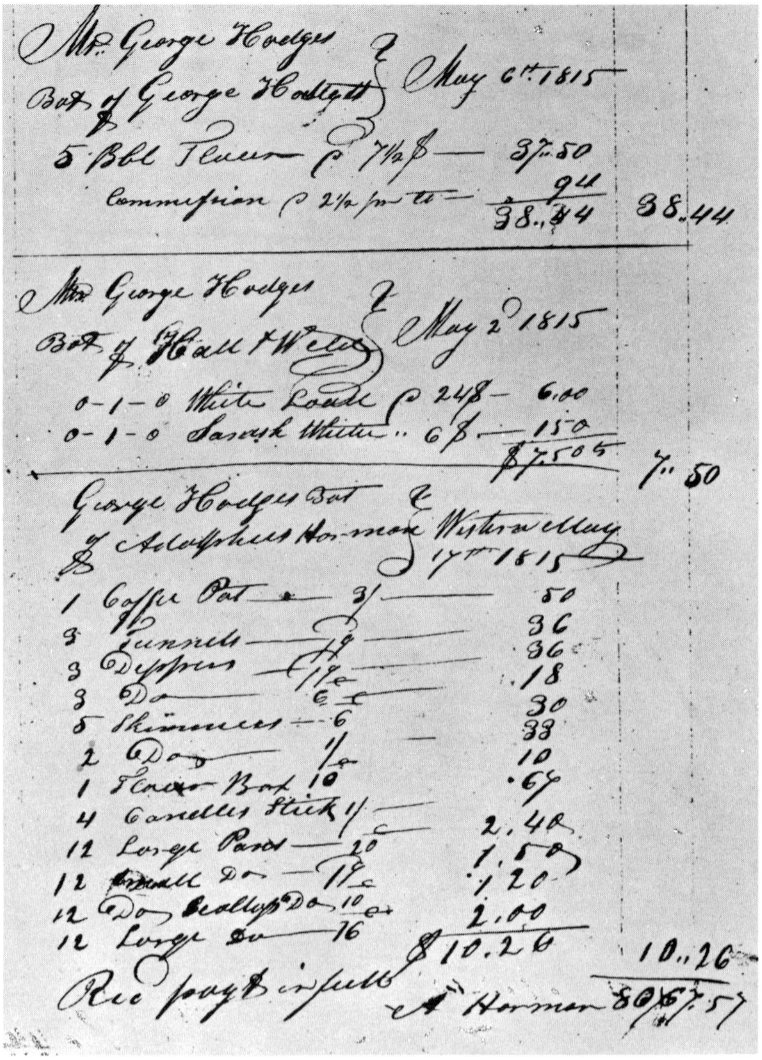

Mr. George Hodges
Bot. of George Hastett    May 6th 1815

5 Bbl Flour @ 7½$ — 37..50
Commission @ 2½ pr ct — ...94
                        38..44   38.44

Mrs George Hodges
Bot. of Hall & Wells    May 2d 1815

0-1-0 White Lead @ 24$ — 6.00
0-1-0 Spanish White .. 6$ — 1.50
                        $7.50    7..50

George Hodges Bot.
of Adolphus Homan Westren May
                        17th 1815

1 Coffee Pot — 3/ — 50
3 Funnels — 1/ — 36
3 Dippers — 1/ — 18
3 Do — 6¢ — 30
5 Skimmers — 6 — 33
2 Do — 1/ — 10
1 Flour Box 10 — .69
4 Candles Stick 1/ — 2.40
12 Large Pans — 20 — 1.50
12 Small Do — 11¢ — 1.20
12 Do Scallop Do 10¢ — 2.00
12 Large Do — 16 — 10.26
                    $10.26   10..26
Recd pay in full
                    A Homan

Plate 193. *List of tin articles and prices paid by George Hodges to Adolphus Homan (?) in the early 19th century when tin was very inexpensive. (Kauffman Collection)*

a device to wire the edges of vessels was issued to James Redheffer of Bridgeton, New Jersey, March 6, 1835, and Edward Converse of Southington, Connecticut patented a seaming machine on November 19, 1833.

The best-known and most successful inventor engaged in this line of work was Seth Peck, from Connecticut. His first patent was granted in 1819; to this day his name survives

Plate 194. *Tin foot warmer with top and bottom framework of wood, which served as an insulator so that neither the feet nor the floor came in direct contact with the tin.*

in the business of Peck, Stow, and Wilcox, manufacturers of sheet metal machinery at Southington, Connecticut.

The exact nature of Peck's early patents is not known; however, he prospered and within a decade had set up a factory to produce his machinery. Agents for distribution and sale were established throughout New York, New England, Pennsylvania, and the South. In 1831 Mr. Peck took in partners and the company became known as the Seth Peck Company. The organization was changed in 1848, again in 1855, and in 1870 the Peck, Stow, and Wilcox Company was established.

An important ally of the early Peck interests was a business started in Southington, Connecticut in 1834. The Stow Company made brass gear wheels and other parts for the Seth Peck Company. This business became a joint stock corporation in 1852 under the name of S. Stow Manufacturing Com-

Plate 195. *Pierced tin foot warmer decorated with typical Pennsylvania motifs. This one probably never had a wooden frame inasmuch as the handle is attached directly to the tin portion of the warmer.*

pany. In 1870 it became a part of the Peck, Stow, and Wilcox Company.

Despite the merging of the Stow Company with their strongest competitors, their line of products continued to bear the Stow name. The 1886 catalogue of Hall and Carpenter, Philadelphia suppliers of tinsmiths tools and machines, lists the following merchandise as Stow products:

1. Patent adjustable bar folder
2. Adjustable bar folder
3. Grooving machines
4. Brass mounted grooving machines
5. Encased wiring machines
6. Setting down machine
7. Large turning machine
8. Burring machine
9. Double seaming machine
10. Beading machine
11. Stove pipe former
12. Patent tube former
13. Gutter beader
14. Power squaring shears

The catalogue lists other interesting machinery to fabricate objects that are usually considered to have been made completely by hand. Among these machines are the tin cup, the candle mold, and the tube former, as well as Miller's Patent Wire bail former. Most of these were invented before the Civil War and were originally operated by hand; by 1886 many of the larger ones were converted to water power or steam. Some of the smaller type are still used today and are operated by hand power.

Plate 196. *Tin pie safe with star and George Washington motifs on the panels. While the star design is quite common, the bust of Washington with his birth and death dates is probably unique. (Courtesy of Guest Antiques)*

Plate 197. *Tin egg beater of the late 19th century.* *(Kauffman Collection)*

that the trade was a large one and produced a great variety of ware. These articles are usually classified according to the use made of them in different areas, such as the laundry and the bakery, and for cooking, lighting, and heating purposes. Because the limitation of space in this survey does not permit a detailed treatment of all areas, the objects will be divided into two groups—plain tinware and decorated tinware.

The advertisements of tinsmiths and the surviving examples indicate that at least ninety per cent of all tinware made was of the undecorated type. As a matter of fact, the writer has never seen an advertisement for decorated tinware. The objects were usually made in geometric forms such as round, square, rectangular, half-round, or elliptical.

The tinsmith was able to compete with machine production longer than any other craftsman who worked in iron. Most of them eventually became plumbers, but they continued to make and repair household articles until the middle of the twentieth century. The current interest in handicrafts has reactivated some tinsmiths; they are making such objects as sconces, chandeliers, lanterns, measures, cooky cutters, and cake pans.

The number of objects of tin plate that have survived and the information obtained by a study of tinsmithing make it evident

Plate 198. *Manufactured tin coffee pot of the late 19th century having a spout made from two pieces of stamped tin soldered together. The iron handle, probably cast, was designed to reduce the conduction of heat from the main body of the pot. (Courtesy of Bradley Antiques)*

Plate 199. *Page from the 1880 catalog of Hall and Carpenter, Philadelphia. The enumeration of items is interesting, particularly the cake cutters, now usually referred to as cookie cutters. (Kauffman Collection)*

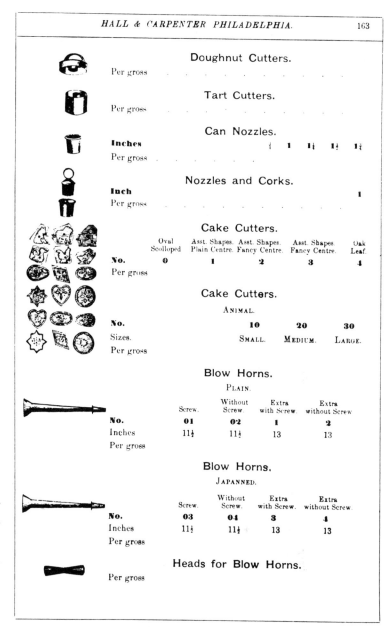

Every tinsmith had his stock of patterns hanging on a nail or on a wire line, where they were easily available. Some of these patterns have survived from the nineteenth century and are interesting relics of the trade. The tinsmith first traced the design of the pattern on a piece of tin plate, and then carefully cut it out with tin snips. To make a large piece of tinware, a number of pieces were joined together because the standard size of the plate was never very large. Even today it is only 22″ × 28″. The craftsman shaped the patterns by using hammers, mallets, rollers, seamers, and so forth. In the eighteenth century this work was done by hand, but later the previously-mentioned small machinery was used. Because tin plate was a cheap and flexible medium, there were rapid changes in the style and function of objects made of this material. Early pieces of tinware are more interesting than the later products because they show evidence of originality on the part of the maker and lack the uniformity that factory-made spouts,

handles, and ears impart to those of the nineteenth century.

There were, of course, regional differences in the products of the tinsmiths. The exten-

Plate 200. *Man-on-a-horse cookie cutter from Pennsylvania. Other popular designs were of eagles, roosters, fish, indians, rabbits, etc. They range in heighth from three to fifteen inches. (Kauffman Collection)*

sive use of the fireplace in New England created a greater need for hearth equipment there than in Pennsylvania, where iron stoves were used as early as 1750. Candlestands with conical tin bases were widely used in New England, while Pennsylvanians favored the tin Betty lamps. The cooky cutter of tin plate was also very popular in Pennsylvania, where they were made in sizes ranging from a height of a few inches to as many as ten or twelve. There were other specialities of each locality; however, the whole business of tinsmithing was more uniform than that of other trades because the lightweight utensils were shipped or peddled all over the eastern seaboard, and in the Northwest Territory as well. A special type of wagon was built for the tin peddler, equipped with many compartments for the small objects, while the large ware dangled over the sides and rear of the vehicle.

It would be impossible to enumerate all of the items made by the hundreds of tinsmiths who worked over a span of at least two hundred and fifty years. The most comprehensive listing known was published in the *Federal Gazette* (Philadelphia) by Thomas Passmore on November 30, 1793. He named seventy-six pieces which he manufactured and concluded by saying that there were other items too numerous to mention. A unique feature of his advertisement was the alphabetical arrangement of the listings, with all but seven of the letters of the alphabet accounted for:

| | |
|---|---|
| Ale tasters | Ovens |
| Argyles for gravy | Oil pumps |
| Boxes for writing | Pots and measures |
| Bathing machines | Plate warmers |
| Bread baskets | Punch strainers |
| Cranes | Powder cannisters |
| Cheese trays | Pepper boxes |
| Cream skimmers | Pudding pots |
| Cheese toasters | Patty pans |
| Cheese ovens | Saucepans |
| Coffee biggins | Speaking trumpets |
| Coffee pots | Sugar boxes |
| Chocolate pots | Snuff boxes |
| Cullenders | Suet strainers |
| Candle boxes | Slicers |
| Candle safes | Scollops |
| Candle molds | Salvanonies |
| Candle sticks | Soup ladles |
| Cannisters | Stills |
| Covers for plates | Staves suitable for ladies |
| Dust pans | Tureens |
| Dripping pans | Tinder boxes |
| Dressing boxes | Ventilators |
| Egg slicers | Water pots |
| Extinguishers | Jugs and tumblers |
| Flour boxes | Kettles |
| Fish kettles | Knife trays |

Plate 201. *Late 19th century tin cannister with a japan finish. Two gold bands are the only decoration on this piece. (Kauffman Collection)*

Plate 202. *Late 19th century spice box with japan background and decoration in gold. Although such objects are attractive, the charm of the earlier decoration has entirely disappeared. (Kauffman Collection)*

| | |
|---|---|
| Funnels | Lanthorns |
| Fenders | Lamps of all kinds |
| Garden engines | Moulds for blomonges |
| Gingerbread cutters | Milk strainers |
| Graters | Money boxes |
| Hash dishes | Meat skreens |
| Hearing trumpets | Milk pails |
| Ice cream pots | Milk saucepans |
| Jacks | |

Although the largest proportion of tinware made in America was of the plain type, the decorated group attracts the most attention today. The most common surviving type is called "japanned ware."

The technique of japanning was imported from Europe, where it reached a high state of development in the eighteenth century. An account of the work in England appears in *Pontypool and Usk Japanned Ware* by W. G. John. Sir Charles Hanbury-Williams, as early as 1732, reported that "To mAllgood has found a new way of japanning which I think so beautiful that I'll send you a couple pieces of it." On July 4th, 1763, an advertisement in the *Glouster Journal* told that "all sorts of the real and most durable Japan Ware is continued to be made and sold at the Manufactory at Pontypool." On August 8th of the same year, a company announced in the same newspaper that "...they have removed their manufactory from Pontypool

to Usk, in Monmouthshire, where they may be furnished with every article in the Japan Way, well known and allowed by Judges far to excel any Performance of the kind in the Known World."

The work done at Pontypool and Usk differed from the type of work done in America. The tin forms on which japanning was practised were objects used in elegant city homes. Many resembled forms made of

Plate 203. *Tin coffee pot decorated with Pennsylvania folk art motifs. Some of this type were signed and dated. Many were made by a man named Ueble and bore dates ranging from 1830 to 1850. (Kauffman Collection)*

Plate 204. *Decorated tin coffin tray with inner panel of amber spatter design, a pattern difficult to execute and rarely found on reproduction work. (Kauffman Collection)*

silver, particularly the Pontypool chestnut urns. There were also snuff boxes, japanned waiters, tea kitchens, dressing boxes and some very elaborately decorated knife boxes.

There is documentary evidence that at least one Englishman came to America to teach japanning. His advertisement in the *Boston Gazette,* July 9-16, 1739, states:

John Waghorne will teach Ladies to Japan in the newest Method invented for that purpose which exceeds all other Japanning for beauty. He has had the honour to teach several Ladies of first quality in England who all did express the greatest Satisfaction for that agreeable and delightful Art.

It is quite probable that the first objects japanned and decorated in America closely resembled the work done earlier in Europe. If any of these have survived, it would be very difficult to declare them either American or European. However, it is evident that schools of tin decorating were gradually set up here and some of their products are obviously indigenous to America.

It is the considered opinion of the majority of experts that most of the American tinware extant today was decorated in the nineteenth century. Since virtually none of the pieces was signed by the person who decorated them, attributions are usually made on circumstantial evidence.

Unlike its European counterpart, American tinware is usually referred to as "country tin." There were no forms to compare to the elaborate chestnut urns of Pontypool or the extravagantly decorated knife boxes from the same area. The japanned background was not always baked to insure permanency; the backgrounds of a number of pieces were simply painted in black, green, yellow, and red. It should be noted that objects with red backgrounds are relatively scarce, while ones with backgrounds in yellow and green are even more rare.

Unfortunately, little is known about the background finishes and the colors used to decorate tin in the earliest times in America. Such information was then regarded as trade secrets, and was only passed by word of mouth from master to apprentice. If a record was made, on scrap paper or in a day book, it has been lost or destroyed by this time.

This atmosphere of secrecy was apparently broken down later, for the 1886 catalogue of Hall and Carpenter, Philadelphia, merchants in tinware and tools to make it, includes directions for making japan varnishes of all colors. The directions for black are as follows:

Black Grounds.—Black grounds for japans may be made by mixing ivory-black with shellac-varnish; or, for coarse work, lampblack and the top coating of common seed-lac varnish. A common black japan may be made by painting a piece of work with drying oil (oil mixed with lead), and putting the work into the stove, not too hot, but of such a degree, gradually raising the heat and keeping it up for a long time, so as not to burn the oil and make it blister. This process makes very fair japan, and requires no ploishing.

Directions were also included in the catalogue for making blue, scarlet, yellow, green, orange, purple, and transparent japans. The transparent type was used to cover a special texture created on the surface of the tin called crystallized tin plate, a process which has defied the ingenuity of all modern decorators of tinware in their attempts to reproduce it. The Hall and Carpenter catalogue also includes directions for producing this texture, as follows:

### CRYSTALLIZED TIN PLATE

Crystallized tin plate has a variegated primrose appearance; it is produced upon the surface of tin plate by applying to it, in a heated state, some diluted nitro-muriatic acid for a few seconds, then washing it with water, drying, and coating it with lacquer. The figures are more or less beautiful and diversified, according to the degree of heat and relative dilution of acid. Place the tin plate, slightly heated, over a tub of water, and rub its surface with a sponge dipped in a liquor composed of four parts of aquafortis, and two of distilled water, holding one part of common salt or sal ammoniac in solution. Whenever the crystalline spangles seem to be thoroughly brought out, the plate must be immersed in water, washed either with a feather or a little cotton (taking care not to rub off the film of tin that forms the feathering), forthwith dried with a low heat, and coated with lacquer varnish; otherwise it loses its lustre in the air. If the whole surface is not plunged at once into cold water, but if it be partially cooled by sprinkling

water on it, the crystallization will be finely variegated with large and small figures. Similar results will be obtained by blowing cold air through a pipe on the tinned surface, while it is just passing from the fused to the solid state.

This crystallized texture was most frequently used on the centers of trays. A great variety of shapes and sizes was made and decorated—round, oval, square, octagonal, rectangular, and the very popular coffin shape; box forms followed the same general shapes. Decorations were also applied to tea caddies, cannisters, coffee pots, measures, mugs, sugar and cream containers, match boxes, and toys. Objects that required frequent washing, such as a nursing bottle, were never decorated; lamps and sconces, rarely.

The subjects used by the country tinsmiths were also different from those favored by sophisticated European decorators. His-

*Plate 205. Tin coffee pot with japan background and decorative motifs in yellow. Such profuse use of yellow is uncommon in the decorated tinware of Pennsylvania.*

GEO. V. KEEN.                    JAS. S. HAGERTY.

## G. V. KEEN & CO.
### HOUSE KEEPERS' EMPORIUM
AND
# TIN WARE MANUFACTORY,

Wholesale and Retail,

*No. 12 BALTIMORE ST.,*

6 doors W. of the Bridge.

Keep constantly on hand an extensive assortment of House Keeping articles of every description.

Hardware, Cutlery, Tin, Sheet Iron and Japanned Ware, Brittania, Block Tin, Willow and Wooden Ware, Etherial and common Oil Lamps, and a variety of fancy goods suitable for House Keepers.

Purchasers are invited to call and examine our stock, as we are prepared to offer great inducements.

Country Merchants in want of TIN WARE, will find a large assortment of our own manufacture, and at very low prices.

## BATH TUBS,
### Shower Baths,
### HIP SPONGE,
AND
### FOOT BATHS,

Refrigerators, and Water Coolers,

Bathing apparatus of all kinds made to order and put up at short notice.

Plate 206. *Advertisement in an 1850 Baltimore business directory showing styles of tinware popular at that time. Curiously, it includes a punched tin lantern, usually regarded as an 18th century product. (Kauffman Collection)*

torical scenes were virtually never used on trays in America, and the very elaborate bird and flower arrangements were used sparingly, if ever. The motifs were usually taken from nature; flowers, fruit leaves, and birds seem to have been special favorites. The common procedure on trays was to place a grouping of flowers or fruits in the center, and decorate the edges with a vine or leaf design. Pennsylvania motifs were usually bold and colorful, while those used in New England were more refined and delicately rendered. Decorators often applied a light gray or white band near the edge of such objects as mugs, coffee pots, and trays, and then painted attractive patterns in green, red, and yellow on them.

Designs were applied by both the free-hand and stencil techniques. Possibly the gifted painters used the free-hand method, while the less talented used stencils. Such a conclusion must be qualified, however, since observation has shown that the use of stencils does not restrict a decorator who has imagination and skill in the use of tools. Since the stencil technique was better suited to the more recent mass production of decorated tinware, little free-hand decoration was done after the period of the Civil War in America.

A technique called piercing was also used to decorate tinware in the nineteenth century. Pieces were cut from patterns in the usual way and a design was drawn on one side of the sheet. The tin plate was then supported on a sheet of lead, or other similar substance, and cuts were made through it at regular intervals along the lines of the de-

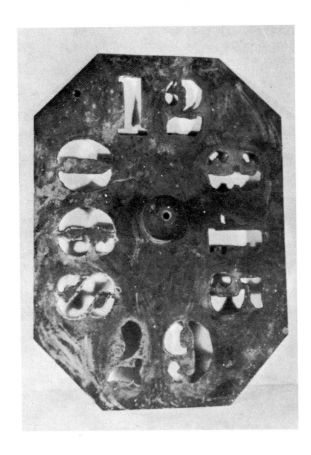

Plate 207. *Tin stencil with handle of wood, typical of the stencils used by farmers and millers throughout the 19th and early 20th centuries. (Kauffman Collection)*

they permitted oxygen to enter so the candle could burn, and they allowed a dim light to be shed by the lantern. On objects such as pie safes, the cuts permitted air to circulate through the storage space, and on cheese molds the excess liquid was drained off through the cuts in the tin plate. The well-known foot warmers of the eighteenth and early nineteenth centuries were cut so that a small quantity of heat could escape and warm the surrounding area.

A technique less well-known than piercing, and used principally in Pennsylvania in the mid-nineteenth century, was called punch-work. The procedure was similar to that in piercing, except that round marks were made with a dull punch on the surface of the metal without completely breaking through the surface. Punch-work created a raised design on the exterior of the vessel on which it was used. The scarcity of surviving objects suggests that very few used this process. Of those who did, many did not sign their pieces, fewer dated them, and only a very small number indicated the name of the person for whom the object was made. The items most frequently decorated in this

sign. Considerable skill was required to execute this technique, for each cut had to be properly located and each impact of the hammer on the chisel had to be made with uniform pressure. Such precision was necessary to make all the openings equal in size.

This procedure in decorating tinware was particularly attractive, for it was both decorative and useful. The openings in the so-called "Revere" lanterns were made in this manner. The cuts formed an interesting design on the outer surface of the lantern,

Plate 208. *Pierced tin cheese mold in the shape of a heart. The openings are not only decorative but also are functional, allowing excessive liquid to drain from the cheese. (Kauffman Collection)*

**147 ✦ THE TINSMITH**

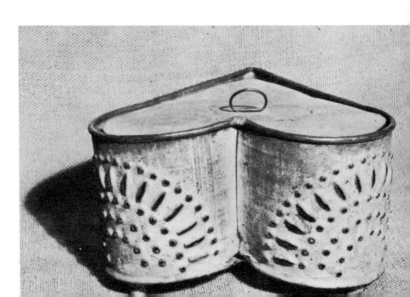

Plate 209. *Unusual tin lid on an American pewter porringer. The lid fits perfectly and bears some stylistic relevance to the porringer. (Kauffman Collection)*

centuries are now mass-produced from aluminum, which is relatively cheap and very durable. The era of the tin cup on the pump is gone forever!

## BIBLIOGRAPHY

BISHOP, J. LEANDER, *A History of American Manufactures from 1608 to 1860.* 2 vols. Philadelphia: Edward Young & Co., 1861.

BRAZIER, ESTHER STEVENS. *Early American Decoration.* Springfield: Pond-Eckberg Co., 1947.

DOW, GEORGE FRANCIS. *Domestic Life in New England in the Seventeenth Century.* Topsfield, Mass.: Perkins Press, 1925.

GOULD, MARY EARLE. *Antique Tin & Tole Ware.* Rutland: Charles E. Tuttle Company, 1958.

JOHN, W. D. *Pontypool and Usk Japanned Wares.* Newport, Mon. England: The Ceramic Book Co., 1953.

KAUFFMAN, HENRY J. *Early American Copper, Tin, and Brass.* New York: Medill McBride Co., 1950.

POWERS, BEATRICE FARNWORTH and FLOYD, OLIVE. *Early American Decorated Tinware.* New York: Hastings House, 1957.

manner were coffee pots, spice boxes, and candle sconces.

Few objects of any type are made of tin plate today, for the twentieth century has produced a highly industrialized economy that has other materials and little room for a handicraftsman working in tin plate. A few tinsmiths have survived because they have added side-lines, such as plumbing and heating; however, their tinwork is largely of a repair nature. Most of the utensils made from tin plate in the eighteenth and nineteenth

Plate 210. *Toy A B C plate of tin, very common in the late 19th century throughout America. They have considerable charm even though machine-made. (Kauffman Collection)*

# Index